MISSION TO THE LORD SOPHY OF PERSIA

E.J.W. GIBB MEMORIAL TRUST

Mission to the Lord Sophy of Persia (1539-1542)

MICHELE MEMBRÉ

Translated with Introduction and Notes by

A.H. MORTON

Former Senior Lecturer in Persian, School of Oriental and African Studies, University of London

PUBLISHED BY THE TRUSTEES OF THE GIBB MEMORIAL

1999

First published by the School of Oriental and African Studies at the University of London 1993

ISBN 0 906094 43 7

British Library Cataloguing-in-Publication Data
A catalogue record of this book is available from the British Library

Printed and published in England for the E.J.W. Gibb Memorial Trust by Aris & Phillips Ltd, Teddington House, Warminster, Wiltshire BA12 8PQ

CONTENTS

To my Mother and Father

INTRODUCTION

The description of his mission to the court of Shah Ṭahmāsp I of Persia left by the Venetian Michele Membré is one of the most informative as well as the most individual of the few European accounts of sixteenth-century Persia. Its author had exceptional opportunities to observe Safavid court society, and recorded his adventures and observations in a brief but lively narrative. The translation is intended to make Membré's work accessible to a wider readership than it can attract in the original Italian, an Italian moreover which, though to some extent normalized in the printed edition, still contains many Venetian features and other peculiarities. Membré presented his *Relazione* to the Collegio of Venice in July 1542, but his mission was later forgotten. The surviving papers, including the single manuscript of the *Relazione*, which is written in several hands, were in a portion of the Venetian archives which was for a period removed to Austria and was only returned to the Archivio di Stato in Venice after 1866, when Venice became part of United Italy. They were not used by the early archival historians of the city, notably Berchet, whose account of Venetian-Persian relations, published in 1865 and still useful, totally ignores Membré. The *Relazione* was first mentioned in print by Bonelli in 1910, first used to any serious extent by von Palombini (1968) and published at last in 1969 in an edition by G.R. Cardona, with an introductory study by G. Scarcia and supplementary material provided by other scholars.

It was Venetian practice for envoys to present such accounts after their missions had ended. They were distinct from despatches, being intended to supply background information rather than report on the progress of negotiations. Several of Membré's letters and other documents concerning his mission also survive. The two Persian letters he brought back have been published several times and are translated in the Appendix. The remaining items are still unpublished and the longest and most important of the despatches is in very poor condition. This last, sent from Lisbon on 17 October 1542, was a copy of an earlier letter of 31 August, only two days after Membré's ship had arrived, which itself seems never to have reached Venice. These are evidently the letters alluded to in the *Relazione*, where they are described as containing details of Membré's audiences with Ṭahmāsp and his departure from the Persian court. It does not appear that there was any communication between him and the Venetian authorities between the time when he left Venetian territory and his arrival in Portugal on the return journey. In the absence of published texts reliance is here placed on Scarcia and to a lesser extent von Palombini for the contents of these documents. The account of Membré's later life is also largely based on that of Scarcia.

* * *

Membré was more messenger than ambassador. His task was to deliver a letter from the Doge which urged the Shah to come to the assistance of Venice and her allies in their war against Ottoman Turkey by attacking the Sultan from the east. This scheme of encouraging the rulers of Persia to open a new front and take the Muslim powers of the Mediterranean region in the rear had attracted Western Europe for centuries. In the thirteenth and fourteenth centuries the Popes and the Crusaders had negotiated with the Ilkhans to this purpose, and, later, Tīmūr's conquests in Syria and Anatolia and his victory over the Ottoman Sultan Bāyazīd (1402), though achieved without Western-European co-operation, had shown that intervention from the direction of Persia could indeed dramatically alter the balance of power close to Europe. With the rapid recovery of the Ottomans, their conquest of Constantinople and their further expansion in the West, the dream of the eastern alliance lost none of its allure. We now know that the grand alliance never came off, but at the time it offered the chance, if it were to work, of spectacular success. And even if the chances of gaining major advantages were realized to be slight, negotiations with Persia were a gambit that always had to be considered. Ottoman awareness of possible insecurity in the rear would itself operate to the benefit of Christian Europe and was therefore worth fostering. Venice, in particular, had pursued such a policy vigorously, though without much success, in the later fifteenth century, in the days of Uzun Ḥasan Āqquyūnlū, whom she had tried to support in his contest against Mehmet II in Anatolia.

In some respects a similar alliance with the Safavids must have looked more promising The religious changes brought about in Persia by the first Safavid Shah, Ṭahmāsp's father Ismā'īl (r. 1501-1524), placed that country in an attitude of permanent hostility towards the majority Sunnī Muslims, of whom the Ottoman Sultans claimed the leadership. In addition, a large proportion of the most effective supporters of the Safavid Shahs were Turks, originating from what was, or had by the time of Ṭahmāsp become, Ottoman territory. Furthermore, Shāh Ṭahmāsp himself had recent reasons for hostility towards Sulṭān Sulaimān. The latter had in 1533-1535 mounted, and himself partly led, a long campaign against the Safavid lands which had resulted in major territorial losses for Ṭahmāsp, including that of Baghdad, and which at one point seemed about to destroy the Safavid state. On the other hand, the difficulties of communicating with Persia had increased. Even in the fifteenth century it had not been easy: Ottoman activity had made it impossible to transport the men and munitions intended for Uzun Ḥasan further than the coast of Cilicia. Since then further Ottoman expansion, most importantly the conquest of Syria and Egypt, had placed the whole Eastern Mediterranean coast under Ottoman control. The Ottoman-Persian frontier had also been pushed eastwards. Membré himself took the Black Sea route but it could not be travelled openly: Kaffa was an Ottoman possession, the Crimea as a whole an Ottoman dependency. The only regularly practicable way to Persia from Western Europe that was not blocked by the Ottomans was the sea route via the Indian Ocean. Membré came back this way: it had the disadvantages of being uncertain, very slow and dependent on Portuguese goodwill. And even the Indian Ocean, at this time of maximum Ottoman expansion, was the scene of Turkish naval operations.

The conclusion of the Persian campaign of 1533-1535 allowed Sulaimān to turn his attention again to the complications of Europe. Among the major powers, Francis I of France had long been cultivating the Sultan's friendship as a counter to the pressure of the Habsburgs, the Emperor and King of Spain Charles V and his brother Ferdinand of Austria. A new factor was the increased effectiveness of the Ottoman fleet, which had recently been placed under the command of the Algerian corsair Barbarossa. Sulaimān and Francis had hopes of acting in combination against the Habsburgs around the Mediterranean, though this was not in fact achieved. In 1537 Southern Italy was subjected to severe raids by the Ottoman fleet, but when the Sultan arrived with his army at Valona on the coast of the Adriatic, instead of making the crossing to Italy as initially intended, in August he attacked the island of Corfu, a Venetian possession. This move made it clear that the peace between Venice and Turkey which had lasted since 1503 was at an end. Venice was in a difficult position in this period. She lacked the resources to compete with the major powers on equal terms; her prosperity depended in great measure on trade, which could only be successfully pursued with Ottoman permission; even the food of the city was partly imported from the Ottoman Empire. She had long enjoyed the goodwill of Sulaimān's influential vizier, Ibrāhīm Pāshā, but in 1536 he had fallen from favour and been executed. Sulaimān had been pressing Venice to join the alliance with France, and there were those in Venice who appreciated the possible advantages. However, their opponents had prevailed. Minor incidents had provided the Sultan with something of a *casus belli*.

Reacting swiftly to the outbreak of open hostilities, as early as 10 October the Council of Ten at Venice took the decision to send messengers to the Sophy, as the Shah of Persia was known, to try to bring him into the war. On 3

November it was resolved to instruct the Governor of Cyprus to see that a letter reached the Sophy by the quickest and surest means. The projected mission to Persia is next mentioned in a cipher letter from Cyprus dated 12 May 1538. The difficulty of finding a capable person willing to undertake the dangerous enterprise had caused delay, but an Armenian had at last been found. In Europe meanwhile, progress had been made in co-ordinating the response to the Ottoman, and French, threat. Largely at the initiative of the Pope (Paul III), a Holy League had been brought into existence, by which the Pope, Venice, Charles V and Ferdinand of Austria agreed to act in concert against the Sultan and Francis I. The treaty had been signed in February. A letter dated 29 August instructs the Governor of Cyprus to send 'once again' a suitable and trustworthy messenger to the Shah. This seems to confirm that the Armenian had set off; his fate is not known. The search for the second messenger seems once more to have been difficult, nor is this surprising, for the Ottomans did not show mercy to enemy agents who fell into their hands. Memory of the affair of Andrea Morosini, the wealthy Venetian consul in Aleppo, would have been fresh. In 1531 he had been dragged behind a horse and then impaled, for giving assistance to an envoy of the Emperor on his way to the Safavid court. In any case, it was not until February 1539 that Membré received his commission.

* * *

Of Membré's origins and early life we know only what emerges from the *Relazione*. In 1539 he was thirty years of age; he was born then in 1509. His family was Venetian and he claimed to be of gentle birth, but, although the Persian court in its letters spoke of him as the descendant of amirs, he was not of patrician rank. The family had been settled in Cyprus for some time. He told Ṭahmāsp that his mother and father were alive and that he had a brother. The Shah must surely have enquired after his own children; his silence on the point indicates that he was not married. As far as is known he remained unmarried throughout his long life. He was a merchant, in a fairly small way of business, and had been so employed, it seems, for all his adult life. He was making, or so at least he told the Governor of Cyprus, some 150 ducats a year. He was related to the Benedetti family, prosperous landowners as well as merchants. He had their patronage, and had been employed by them on trading voyages to Turkey and Syria. In the latter country he had spent some time in Damascus.

It was his knowledge of languages that above all qualified Membré for the mission to Persia. Bernardo Benedetti, who had been commissioned to find a suitable envoy, specified that the person he was searching for needed to know Turkish. Nor is this surprising in the context of a mission to Persia, for the main language of communication at the court of Persia in the Safavid period was Turkish. It was the mother tongue of the Shahs, although they knew Persian as well, and it was the Turkish-speaking element of the population which was dominant. Membré's Greek was good enough for him to pass among Greeks as an Athenian, as he says he did in Turkey, and it is most likely that he acquired such a degree of fluency as a child. He was literate in Greek: for no obvious reason a handful of names and other words are provided with transcriptions in Greek script in the *Relazione*. Thus he was evidently able to read the Greek psalter in which the letter from the Doge to the Sophy was concealed. Beside Italian, Greek and Turkish, Membré evidently knew Arabic. He is credited with knowing it at a later period by Ramusio and he would have had the opportunity to learn it during his journeys to Syria. Though in the *Relazione* the only necessarily Arabic phrases quoted are standard religious formulae, it was presumably his ability to talk to them in Arabic that encouraged him, while in Persia, to take a Moor, or Muslim, from Tunis and a second Moor into his service. Ramusio also includes a knowledge of Persian among Membré's talents, and with his help obtained information from Persian merchants in Venice. However, whether Membré really knew much Persian is uncertain. The Persian merchants would have known Turkish, the language which Membré principally required for his position as Dragoman. The Persian language is never mentioned in the *Relazione* and the few phrases in it which can securely be identified as Persian are again formulaic. Nearly all the exotic terms he uses in describing Persia, whatever their language of origin, are to be found in the Persian texts of the period, but, with a few exceptions, they would have been current in both Persian and the Turkish spoken in Iran. That Membré did in fact acquire most of them through Turkish is confirmed by his occasionally giving them, not in their simple, absolute forms but with Turkish suffixes still attached (e.g. *nafti*, *sufrachissi*), and sometimes by the precise form of his transcriptions. (In the translation a transliteration system appropriate to Arabic and Persian has been used, except in a few cases, mostly where Turkish syntax is involved, and even in these the complication of different forms for the consonants has been avoided.)

Membré had a talent for languages; his Turkish was good enough to enable him to acquire detailed information of many kinds. His transcription of foreign names and words is not systematic, but there are not many points where it is still uncertain what he meant. One notable feature for a native speaker of Italian (or Greek) is his unfailing ability to perceive the sound h. On the other hand, his linguistic knowledge was not precise or at all bookish. It is evident from the cases mentioned above that he did not fully understand the nature of Turkish suffixes, and though Bombaci states that his translations from Turkish in his later years are good, Ménage, in his study of the supposed Map of Ḥājjī Aḥmad, has shown convincingly that his knowledge of the Arabic script was poor and his attempts to write Turkish in it full of mistakes. Even the Italian of the *Relazione* is rather rough, most obviously to a foreigner with its constantly repeated conjunctions and the laboured, perhaps mercantile, precision of its use of '*ditto*' ('aforementioned' or 'said'). The opening passages, which attempt a higher style, are rather awkward. Membré's linguistic gift was essentially practical and oral. He was a sociable man, who found it easy to get to know people, even if, by his own testimony, his sociability was often deployed to gain his own ends. His bent for mimicry can be exemplified for Portuguese. He tells us that he could not understand that language when he arrived at Hormuz, but it must have been largely through Portuguese that he acquired his information about India and the vocabulary of the *Relazione* shows a distinct Portuguese tinge, especially in the final section.

* * *

The main text of the original *Relazione* has no subdivisions. It has been divided into eight chapters in the translation, but also falls into three main sections, the first describing the journey to Persia (Chapters 1-2), the second, the heart of the book, covering the period of Membré's stay at the Persian court (Chapters 3-6) and the third largely dealing with the return journey to Europe, but also including a description of Tabriz, the Shah's capital (Chapters 7-8). The story begins with his commissioning by the Governor of Cyprus, ponderously told in the attempt to produce an ingratiating effect on the Signory, the Venetian government. It then proceeds more straightforwardly with what was the most obviously perilous part of the journey, the entry into Turkey and the crossing of Anatolia. Here, as throughout, Membré keeps a stiff upper lip. He sometimes mentions the dangers but he does not dwell on them, tending rather to show a humorous pride in his own cleverness at surmounting the obstacles. On 1 March 1539 he set out from Nicosia, with the Signory's letter concealed in the binding of the Greek psalter. The sale of corn, shipped from Larnaca, provided him with a pretext for going to Candy in Crete, where he disguised himself in the clothes of a Greek subject of the Turk. To go on to Chios, an Ottoman dependency, he managed to be issued with a passport as an inhabitant of Chios, and, for the next stage, adopted the identity of the long-lost brother of an Athenian acquaintance in Cyprus. The voyage through the Aegean, in the event completed without incident, was itself extremely dangerous. Large-scale Turkish naval operations in the previous year had reduced most of the Venetian dependencies in the region to submission, but the activity of the Turkish foists reported by Membré shows that the search for plunder and slaves was still continuing. Santorini and Naxos, which he saw, were possessions of the Duke of Naxos, whose family was of Venetian origin, but he had just become an Ottoman tributary. Even the Greeks of Chios, whose Genoese Lords had been under Ottoman suzerainty longer, were not safe from Turkish raiding. It is testimony to the resilience of trade in such situations that henna from captured Turkish ships was already being re-exported from Crete to Chios for subsequent resale to the Turks. What makes Membré's device of passing himself off as a merchant particularly interesting is that his commercial transactions and the stratagems he used to make progress must be of the same kind as those used by merchants in ordinary circumstances.

In April 1539 the Anatolian mainland was reached. Henna was changed for carded cotton at Manisa; the cotton was sold at Karahisar. Presumably no suitable merchandise was to be found there, for a donkey was the only purchase. On it Membré proceeded to Angora where he bought a small supply of the famous mohairs and camlets, fine cloths made from the hair of the Angora goat. These provided him with, as it were, his camouflage as far as Georgia. He was intending to enter Persia by one of the roads through Eastern Anatolia but at Chankiri news now reached him that the Turks had closed the Persian frontier. Not baffled for long, he turned to the Black Sea route. Selling the donkey at the port of Samsun, he took ship for Kaffa in the Crimea. There he was able to make a rapid transfer to a ship going to Georgia. He mentions no formalities as being required to leave Ottoman territory at Kaffa and the rest of the journey to the border with Persia calls for little comment. The pose of merchant continued to serve him well in Mingrelia and the rest of Georgia. Where more conspicuous travellers, Ambrogio Contarini in the fifteenth century and Sir John Chardin in the seventeenth, report being outrageously treated by the inhabitants, Membré has nothing worse to complain of than the mosquitoes.

* * *

On reaching the Persian border fortress of Lori in August (or perhaps July) 1540, Membré revealed his identity to the Captain of the fort. He was provided with a horse and an escort and after a ride of seven days arrived at the Royal encampment near Marand, about 45 miles northwest of the capital city, Tabriz. The scene changes. Instead of muleteers and merchants, he is for almost a year in the society of, friends with, the greatest Lords of the land. It must have been the most remarkable experience of the humble Venetian Cypriot's life and he thoroughly enjoyed it. As was said at the outset, he had exceptional opportunities to observe the Persian court. Ṭahmāsp at first welcomed the prospect of co-operation against the Ottomans, or at least was prepared to give it serious consideration. It was recognized what courage and enterprise Membré had shown in reaching Persia. People admired him for this, and many evidently came to like him. They were able to talk to him in Turkish. The fact that he was alone was a very great advantage. In contrast to the normal ambassador he had no suite to keep him under observation, distract him with their quarrels, or make it necessary for the embassy to be isolated in separate accommodation. On his own he could simply be sent to stay as a guest with one of the courtiers. We are never told whether Membré's first host, Shāh 'Alī Chapnī, had any particular position at court but he held the high rank of Sulṭān and was later made Governor of Van. His host in Tabriz, Shāh qulī Khalīfa, Keeper of the Seals, was one of the most important Ministers. The households of these men must have numbered dozens and dozens of people. But it seems that Membré was treated as a fairly close member of the family. He was invited to social occasions, not only the great public festivals but also more private occasions such as funerals and weddings. He learnt about people's families and even saw and was able to comment on their wives, and their beautiful, big, round pearls. At Tabriz, he tells us, he had the free run of the the houses of all the great Lords, which were scattered in the neighbourhood of the Royal Palace, and stayed with some of them for weeks. And this situation lasted for an unusually long time, the best part of a year. The perceptions of so many travellers are limited by the speed at which they travel. Moreover, and it is one of the unexpected items that emerge from the *Relazione*, the atmosphere in court circles was remarkably open and self-confident. This is more than a reflection of Membré's own sanguine temperament for it can also be explained as truly representing the state of affairs among the particular social group among which he spent most of his time, that of the upper stratum of the Qizilbāsh. His observations on this section of society are one of the most valuable parts of the book particularly because, although they were for long the dominant group in the Safavid state, the Persian literary sources tell us rather little about their way of life.

The term Qizilbāsh is only used once in the *Relazione* (p. 31) but it was already well known in Europe. A Turkish compound, the word means red-headed and was applied to the followers of the Safavids on account of the red cap which they wore. This was first introduced by Ṭahmāsp's grandfather Shaikh Ḥaidar not long before his death in 1488. The style of the cap changed over time, but the generic name was *tāj*, meaning crown. Membré's account, and his sketches, are important for its history (see the figure on p. 26). As a social term Qizilbāsh has had various meanings depending on time and viewpoint but it is generally used by historians, and some Safavid sources, to refer to the largely Turkish and nomadic followers of the early Safavids, and the descendants of the group later.

It was the Qizilbāsh who had provided the religious enthusiasm and military potential which had enabled Ṭahmāsp's father Ismā'īl to become Shah of Persia. To sketch the background very briefly, the Safavid family took its name from Shaikh Ṣafī al-Dīn of Ardabil in Adharbaijan, who achieved some prominence in the early fourteenth century as a Sufi Shaikh, that is as the head and spiritual guide of an order of Muslim mystics. His descendants continued as hereditary leaders of the order, acquiring considerable property in the process. Such organizations were common in the period and were essentially quietist. In the middle of the fifteenth century Shaikh Junaid, Ṭahmāsp's great-grandfather, was expelled from Ardabil in a family dispute over the leadership of the order. He gathered a following among the Turkish nomads of Anatolia, Syria and North-western Persia. Abandoning the conventional Sufism of the earlier Safavid Shaikhs, he made use of the existing heterodox beliefs of the nomads to pursue a militant policy. Central was the belief in a messiah-like leader, regarded as an emanation of the divinity, with a mission to purify the world and entitled to absolute obedience from his followers. At this stage Safavid militancy expressed itself in the form of attacks on non-Muslims, principally in the area of the Caucasus. Junaid himself, and his son Ḥaidar, met their deaths in that region while leading raiding armies of Turcoman followers which came into conflict with the Muslim rulers of Shīrvān.

Shortly before his death in 1460 Junaid had married the sister of the Āqquyūnlū chief Uzun Ḥasan. The latter was shortly to conquer most of Persia and become one of the most important rulers of the region. What led Uzun Ḥasan to accept the marriage is obscure but its benefits for the descendants of Junaid were great: thanks to their links with the royal family they regained control of Shaikh Ṣafī al-Dīn's shrine at Ardabil. Haidar, the son of the Āqquyūnlū princess, was later married to a daughter of Uzun Ḥasan. As has been mentioned, it was under Ḥaidar that the red cap that gave rise to the term Qizilbāsh was introduced. In spite of the ties of blood there was a limit to Āqquyūnlū tolerance of Safavid militancy. Ya'qūb Āqquyūnlū, Uzun Ḥasan's son, had sent reinforcements to the ruler of Shīrvān to help him resist Ḥaidar's marauding army, and the Safavids remained under well-justified suspicion. In 1499 Ḥaidar's son Ismā'īl, aged twelve, emerged from Gilan on the Caspian coastland, where he had taken refuge from Āqquyūnlū pursuit, and gathered a Qizilbāsh following. They were soon turned against the Āqquyūnlū. The Empire of Uzun Ḥasan had been weakened and divided by disputes over the succession, and in the space of a few years Ismā'īl became ruler of most of Persia, Iraq, parts of Eastern Anatolia and even of what is now northwestern Afghanistan. Safavid power was to some extent accompanied by a move towards the acceptance in Persia of Ithnā 'asharī Shi'ism rather than messianic

Qizilbash ideology, but how far this affected the Qizilbāsh, and even Ismā'īl himself is a question that still needs to be decisively answered. It has long been suggested that defeat by the Ottomans at the battle of Chāldirān in 1514 brought an end to Ismā'īl's messianic pretensions, but there is some evidence that they were by no means dead and, as Aubin has now shown clearly, the behaviour of Ismā'īl and his court was highly unorthodox in any Islamic terms right up to the end of the reign. The most conspicious, if not necessarily the most fundamental, feature of this unorthodoxy is the attitude to drinking alchohol. Wine was indulged in among the Qizilbāsh in the reign of Ismā'īl, not shamefacedly and in private as an illegal vice, but openly and with enthusiasm as part of public rituals. The most striking descriptions of these occasions, which were not confined to the King's court, come from the Portuguese (who took their wine diluted with water), but they are well attested in the Persian sources too.

In 1524 António Tenreiro was with the Portuguese embassy entertained at the Naurūz festivities by Ismā'īl just before he died of alchoholic excess. He saw the ten-year old Ṭahmāsp drinking as hard as his father. A few days later he heard reports that the new King had made a show of killing with his own hands lions, bears and men. Obviously the boy was trying at first to fill his awesome father's role of charismatic leader. The years after the accession were chiefly filled with violent disputes among the Qizilbāsh tribes, a succession of the tribal leaders gaining control of the Shah and the resources of the state. This was soon complicated by war with the Uzbeks in the East. Ṭahmāsp himself wrote that he really became King in the summer of 1527, but early Persian sources contradict this. However, there is no doubt that he gradually attained greater power, and it is also clear that he was soon moving away from the pattern set by his father. The influence of the Shī'ī theologians grew. His acquisition of real control can be dated to the crisis of the Ottoman invasion in 1533-1534, and one of the major steps that marked it is the episode of his repentance, that is his abandonment of sinful practices. By his own account the advice given by two apparitions of saintly figures in dreams led to the decision. It was not simply a personal choice. Repentance was also ordained throughout the kingdom, and executions occurred in the course of its enforcement. Nor, though the sources for the event fail to make the point, was it simply a campaign against vice. It was a rejection of the old Qizilbāsh way of life. Among sins henceforth banned were drinking and the use of other intoxicants, by which hashish in particular is meant. Also fornication and sodomy, the latter of which Aubin has shown to have been prevalent during the reign of Ismā'īl. It was a bold stroke, particularly at such a moment, but Membré's account confirms that it was not unsuccessful. The only drinking he notes at court, and it was excessive enough, was that of Bahrām Mīrzā and his entourage, who held their parties in private. At the one he describes in detail there is a noticeable atmosphere of homosexuality. If there was truth in the story of Ṭahmāsp's mother's plot to replace him with Bahrām it presumably represented a desire in some quarters to bring back the good old days.

Ṭahmāsp's repentance represented an important stage in the imposition of the Shi'ite form of Islam on Iran. From later in his reign we possess a brief but important Memoir written by himself. It is an apologetic addressed in the 1560s to Sultan Sulaimān but it reveals how Ṭahmāsp saw himself to be directly guided by a higher world; at important points apparitions of Imams and other saintly figures in dreams had guided him to do right, as in the episode of his repentance. Other sources confirm his preoccupation with religious matters. There is no doubt that he himself had abandoned his forefathers' pretension to messianic status. A band of religious enthusiasts who persisted in maintaining that the Shah was in fact the Mahdī, the 'Messiah' of the Shi'ites, was put to death. We know, as has already been said, that Ṭahmāsp was under the influence of Shī'ī theologians of unimpeachable orthodoxy, yet, as the recent Iranian revolution has shown, orthodox Shī'ī theology is extremely reluctant to confer legitimacy on any ruler in the absence of the Mahdī, preferring to reserve it for the theologians themselves. Expectations that the Mahdī's return was imminent were current in the mid-sixteenth century and in them Ṭahmāsp appears to have found himself a kind of solution to the problem of his own legitimacy, a solution which suited his own reactive rather than aggressive temperament. Above all it is his vowing of his sister to be the Mahdī's bride which indicates the hopes he had. Their disappointment may account to some extent for the withdrawal of his later years.

* * *

The Qizilbāsh notables among whom Membré moved could well remember the practices which had only been banned a few years before. And if ceremonial public drinking-parties were a thing of the past, his account is particularly precious in showing how much of the old way of life still survived. Many, but not all, of its features are recorded elsewhere, but there is no one source that provides such a rich and varied collection of them. A few examples may be noted. The day after he reached the court Membré observed the arrival of a large group of Turcomans, come from as far away as Arzinjan in Turkey to join the Shah. Their shouts of *Allāh, Allāh* as they rode round called upon the leader to show himself to his followers. The leader's acceptance of the suppliants in his service was acknowledged by gifts of cloth and the grant of the *tāj*, whereupon the new Qizilbāsh gave their own presents of animals. They were then allotted territory to settle in. The scene was repeated when Ghāzī

Khān and his following arrived at the camp shortly before Membré's departure. Evidently this was the customary ritual for Qizilbāsh groups aspiring to join the Shah's service. The *tabarrā'īs* who preceded the king and the great men at court cursing the enemies of 'Alī may not themselves have been of Qizilbāsh stock but their presence is one of the most characteristic features of the early Safavid period, and Membré's the fullest description. It went in particular with the strong feeling against the Ottomans which Membré attests elsewhere, in the songs sung at the weddings of the *qūrchīs*, the king's guards, in his conversation with the Sayyids of Uskū, and in the behaviour of the other *tabarrā'īs*, who in the streets of Tabriz reinforced this attitude. Yet, as noted below, if Ṭahmāsp had ever had aggressive designs on Turkey they were at this time being abandoned for an essentially defensive policy. To be affected too by his inaction in this respect, and similarly ignorant of the fact, were the devotees who made the long and dangerous journey from inside Turkey to purchase objects sanctified by contact with their Shah. References to the circulations of such 'relics' are found elsewhere, but it is remarkable to have a European eye-witness account from the heart of things. Perhaps most noteworthy of all is the description of the weddings of the *qūrchīs* and in particular the ceremonial beating which Membré underwent with the other guests. No parallel for the whole episode is known, but the actual beating ceremony, which is wholly un-Islamic, is mentioned occasionally in a curious variety of contexts throughout the Safavid period in Iran and is closely related to ceremonies still current among the Kızılbash or Alevis of Turkey, descendants of groups which once were devoted to the Safavid Shahs. Also worth noting are the descriptions of the great public festivals in Tabriz, with their unorthodox features and the enthusiastic participation of visitors from the villages outside Tabriz, led by their village *khalīfas*. Such village organization has already been mentioned in the neighbourhood of the royal camp. It appears to be wholly unrecorded elsewhere.

Membré's *Relazione* fits worthily into the tradition of the dispassionate observation of foreign events and customs in which Venetian diplomats and merchants were skilled. A few further remarks about his individual style of observation may be made. He was not of patrician descent like the other Venetians who have left accounts of their missions, for instance, Barbaro and Contarini in the fifteenth century, Degl' Alessandri later in the reign of Ṭahmāsp. In comparison with them or with the English merchant Anthony Jenkinson he was not a highly educated man. The contrast is even greater with such sophisticated observers of seventeenth century Persia as Della Valle, Olearius and Chardin. Wholly lacking in his work is any attempt to analyse. There are none of those synoptic statements about, for instance, the Persian army or even the geography of the country. Absent too, and this may be the

Venetian tradition, are both the speculations about the Biblical and Classical past of the Middle East which the more bookish travellers found increasingly fascinating, and any show of interest in the Christian religion. Membré does not mention meeting a single fellow-Christian between leaving the Armenian districts near the Persian border and arriving in Hormuz. God is occasionally acknowledged but nowhere does Membré indicate that the absence of the consolations of religion worried him. If he attended church in Hormuz or Goa he does not tell us. He is above all preoccupied with the visible, the tangible and the practical.

The overall structure of the *Relazione* is extremely effective, but the actual technique of description generally gives something of the impression of a series of snapshots. Within the chronological framework of the journey, which is only occasionally violated, each event or feature is described in a few lines and then the subject changes. The transitions are sometimes abrupt and can seem illogical. There are longer set-pieces, but valuable as they are, the writer evidently did not find them easy to compose. The most elaborate of these are the descriptions of the Royal encampment, the court on the move, the King's palace (particularly obscure) and the city of Tabriz. These are difficult to follow at first, though with reflection they are most often seen to make good sense. The finest example of the awkardness with which these more extensive topics are treated is the opening of the account of the encampment: 'However, to inform your Most Excellent Lordships more particularly, the customs and ways of the court of the said Sophy are of this manner, that is, there was a cord as thick as a finger, ...' He is sometimes tempted into digressions. Note, for instance, the passage where, just introduced into the Shah's presence, the culmination of the outward journey, he wanders off to give details of a number of the attendant courtiers, their appearance and habits, their children, even their houses in Tabriz, which he has not yet seen. The entry into the Shah's presence is then briefly repeated. The delivery of the letter has already been mentioned once before this. Here the feeling of pride at having such highly-placed acquaintances is evident. Of course Membré was not writing a polished work of art, he may have written in haste, and some points not in the *Relazione* were no doubt covered in the despatches. The absence of bookish speculation and even analysis, so often unsoundly based or misconceived at this period, can be regarded as helpful rather than the opposite. Though clumsy and jerky at times, the snapshot technique is something of a guarantee of authenticity. Many of Membré's observations are in fact confirmed in one way or another elsewhere. For example, his brief references to local political events are nearly all paralleled in the rather meagre coverage of those years in the Safavid chronicles. (They can be followed up through the biographical notes which follow the translation.) On many important topics his information is unrivalled. There is no account of the Royal encampment in the sixteenth century which comes near to Membré's in its detail. His is the only real description we have of Tabriz at the time when it was the Safavid capital. His information on court life and the Qizilbāsh are probably the most valuable parts of the book.

On the other hand there were important areas of Persian society and even of the organization of the Safavid state which did not attract Membré's attention. Here the fact that he was so well placed among the Qizilbāsh was probably a drawback. Standing in contrast to the largely nomadic and Turkish Qizilbāsh was the settled rural and urban population of the country, largely Persian speaking, for which the not-entirely satisfactory term Tājīk will be used here. From the educated and property-owning upper class of the Tājīks was drawn the personnel required for the functioning of the bureaucratic apects of the state. Of individual Tājīks at court we are only introduced to the equivocal figure of the Chief Minister, Qāḍī-yi Jahān and the buffoonish ones of the Sayyids of Uskū. It is interesting that Membré notes that these people all wore the *tāj*: the distinction between Turk and Tājīk was perhaps not so easy to perceive at court or elsewhere as we like to think. Otherwise the scribes and accountants are not mentioned. The painters remain hidden in their tent. The maker of the fortune-telling clock at Tabriz is the only notable representative of intellectual life. He and the mountebanks in the square are the only people described as Persians. Most conspicuously absent is the clerical class, the judges, theologians and others. There is no doubt that they played an important part in the state even under Ismā'īl and that their influence increased under Ṭahmāsp, but clearly they were not particularly visible to Membré. In spite of the length of his stay in Tabriz, Membré gives little information about the urban population. In most cases the activities he comments on there are those of the Qizilbāsh attached to the court. Even the Persian *cuisine* he describes is stated to be that of the highest class. The only places where the sentiment of the town populace, rather than that of court circles, seems to be reflected are in certain parts of the description of the *'Āshūrā* ceremonies and in the account of the entertainers in the city squares. Curiously, though elsewhere on his journey Membré shows an interest in commercial matters, he says very little indeed about the trade of Tabriz.

Two features of Membré's character deserve to be pointed out, his humour and his interest in money. It is no doubt partly due to lack of experience in high-level diplomacy that a man of his low social position should have revealed them both so clearly in an official report to the Venetian Government, but they were obviously very much a part of him and for us add considerably to the charm of his narrative. The humour is most obvious when concerned, often with partly ironic self-congratulation, with Membré himself. Conspicuous instances include the chicanery by which he managed to pass himself off successively as inhabitant of Chios and citizen of Athens, the description of the pain he felt being ritually beaten at a Qizilbāsh wedding and the fooling of the Captain of Hormuz. It is not surprising that a merchant should have recorded information about trade and such related matters as currency, but a more personal interest in the subject of money is apparent in such episodes as Membré's debate with the Governor of Cyprus about the terms of his employment, and most clearly in the rueful relation of the prediction of the riches coming to him which he received from the fortune-telling clock. Once the humorous and acquisitive tones have been recognized they can be detected in less obvious places, even, surely, combined together, in the account of his arrival at death's door at Terçeira on the return journey, and the discovery of his smuggled jewels by the Portuguese customs.

* * *

In May or June 1540 news reached Ṭahmāsp that a Venetian ambassador was at Constantinople negotiating for peace. The Persian embassy that had been planned was cancelled. Membré was in disgrace. Beyond this the *Relazione* tells us only that in August, with the help of Ghāzī Khān Takkalū, Membré was sent off by the King. In the letters he wrote to Venice after reaching Portugal, however, it seems that a contradictory version of events is given. According to this, the Shah was furious at Venetian duplicity and Membré had to flee the court. Two friends, Shāh Muḥammad and Shāh qulī (Khalīfa?), provided him with false documents, addressed to Charles V, which enabled him to fool the Portuguese into accepting that he was an ambassador of the Emperor as well as of Venice. This is indeed what he says he maintained when questioned by the Captain of Hormuz. A strange account of an undercover mission to Persia given by Correa seems quite likely to refer to Membré. If so, it provides confirmation that the Portuguese accepted him as the Emperor's ambassador. Scarcia was inclined to take the story of the flight from court as substantially true, but it presents considerable difficulties. If Membré was a fugitive, why did he write in the *Relazione* that the Shah had sent him off? Why did the acquaintances from court he met in Isfahan not have him arrested rather than look after him and set him on his way? Why did the Persian ambassadors at Hormuz support his story? Above all, what is to be made of the letter of Shāh Ṭahmāsp (Appendix, No. 2)? It is written after the arrival of the news of the peace negotiations at Constantinople, does reflect the Shah's dissatisfaction, but does not entirely rule out future co-operation. It also states that Membré had been given leave to depart. There seems no reason to consider it false.

The positive Persian reaction to the proposed alliance which was evident at Membré's first audience was maintained for a long period. It is reflected in the letter from Qāḍī-yi Jahān (Appendix, No. 1), which was probably given to Membré at the time when preparations for the return embassy were being made. However, by April, if not earlier, Membré began to feel that he was being unnecessarily delayed. Winter, which might have been a valid reason for postponing departure, was now well over and yet the embassy was not sent off. Ṭahmāsp, with his usual inclination to wait on events, was at this point waiting for news from the West. In his letter he states that Membré's departure was delayed while he waited for confirmation or rebuttal of the rumours of the Venetian peace negotiations. We do not know when the rumours reached him - but the negotiations had begun early in 1539. He was presumably also waiting to see, for one thing, whether the Sultan was intending to attack Persia, and, for another, for evidence of activity on the part of the Holy League. Confirmation that no attack was about to take place and that the League had proved ineffective enabled him to make up his mind that the alliance need not be taken seriously. In spite of the hostility between Persia and Turkey, and how strong it was is attested in the *Relazione* and elsewhere, it is not likely that many people felt, as one of the the Sayyids of Uskū once maintained, that Venetians were better than Turks. The alternative view, that Ottoman aggression against the Christians of Europe was to the benefit of Islam, is well attested in Safavid sources and appears in Ṭahmāsp's own Memoir. Towards the end of the year, after the army's expedition against the Kurd Ḥājjī Shaikh which Membré saw depart, Ṭahmāsp himself went on his first raiding campaign in Christian Georgia. It cannot have lasted long before winter came, but seems almost designed to signal that the Shah had turned away from the idea of alliance with Christian Europe.

Yet, to return to the question of Membré's departure, as has been said above, the Shāh's letter is not wholly negative. Possibly some show of royal displeasure was thought necessary but it seems likely that Membré was given leave to depart, while denied the honour of an audience. That he travelled incognito once again need have had no other reason than a desire to avoid news of his return reaching the Ottomans. Nor is it at all unlikely that he was given messages for Charles V and perhaps even the other partners in the Holy League. Though not commissioned by them, he had effectively represented their interests. As far as Venice herself was concerned, Membré's mission had in fact lost its point before it began. The naval battle of Prevesa (25 September 1538), had shown Venice, whose possessions in the Aegean had already largely succumbed to the Ottoman fleet, that her allies were not likely to exert themselves greatly on her behalf. The first ceasefire negotiations with Turkey had begun at about the time of Membré's departure from Cyprus in 1539, though presumably he was not aware of them. It may have been the embassy early the next year which came to Ṭahmāsp's attention. The formal peace was signed in October 1540. On the other hand, the most formidable of the allies, Spain and Austria, had no reason to make peace. If Ṭahmāsp had any interest in even pretending to continue negotiations it would have been natural for him to try to communicate with the Habsburgs, with whom he had had diplomatic contacts before. The Persian court was not ignorant of the relative status of the European powers and it would have been natural enough to entrust Membré with some message to Charles V. This would also have helped to solve the problem of what to do with Membré. Though Portugal was at the time engaged in its own hostilities against the Sultan's fleet in the Indian ocean, as a Venetian he might have been suspect to the Portuguese as a potential spy for a trading rival; at Hormuz he did in fact fall under suspicion. Some kind of accreditation to Charles V would have made him more acceptable.

If Ṭahmāsp had been of an aggressive nature things might have been very different. Of the partners of the League it was Austria which was both able to act against the Turk and had reason to do so. The year 1541 saw Austria at war with Sulaimān over Hungary and hostilities continued until 1547. During this period Ṭahmāsp was faced with no external threat. The situation was perfect for him to move against Turkey, but in fact he undertook no aggressive action of any scope in any direction. As usual the grand alliance had failed to materialize. The early Safavid interest in conquest in Anatolia had clearly been abandoned; no attempt was even made to recover Baghdad. In 1546 Ṭahmāsp's brother Alqās rebelled and then fled to Turkey. Sulaimān, making use of him, in 1548 turned once again to the East. Ṭahmāsp succeeded in largely holding his own with his usual defensive tactics until in 1555 a long-lasting peace was concluded.

Ṭahmāsp was twenty six when Membré first saw him. The *Relazione* portrays a young and active man, generous to his followers and a good horseman. Audiences were relatively informal: everybody sat down when the king sat. Outside the Harem the Shah was surrounded by *qūrchīs*, *tabarrā'īs* and others. Yet there are signs of the reserved and withdrawn temperament which revealed itself more fully later. The Shah had already rejected the strenuous pleasures of hunting, and preferred the more peaceful pastime of fishing. Others made jokes in his audiences, but he, unlike his father, was serious before foreign envoys. The entertainment of Membré he left to others. The grasping meanness of the the last period of his reign may be foreshadowed by Membré's comment on the high prices charged for the things made holy by his touch, such as shoes and the water he had washed in. It may be accidental but it is appropriate that the *Relazione* contains no description of his personal appearance.

In Ṭahmāsp's later years his reserve became far more pronounced. In 1555, shortly after peace was made with Sulaimān, the capital was removed from Tabriz to Qazvin, some three hundred miles by road to the south-east. The move is usually explained as due to the fact the Tabriz had proved impossible to hold whenever there was an Ottoman invasion, though at the time the move was made this particular danger had receded. In 1557 Ṭahmāsp took up permanent residence in Qazvin, where new palaces were built. He was only in his mid-forties, but he never went on campaign again. A final fishing expedition to nearby Tārum took place in the autumn of 1562. It was marred by the illness of his favourite sister Sulṭānim, the Mahdī's destined bride. She died not long after the return to Qazvin and the shock of losing her no doubt contributed to Ṭahmāsp's further withdrawal. Hopes of the imminent appearance of the Mahdī must also have been called into question, though they were not completely abandoned. Ṭahmāsp does not appear to have left Qazvin again. Foreign and Persian accounts depict him in this later period as bigoted, astonishingly mean and obsessed with the avoidance of pollution and disease. The contrast with the situation observed by Membré, when the court was mobile and the king visible, is great. Like the episode of the repentance from sin, the withdrawal to Qazvin was a move away from early Qizilbāsh practice. Nevertheless, during the nineteen years of his Qazvin period Ṭahmāsp was by no means an ineffective ruler. He was fortunate not to have been faced with any serious foreign threat, but the period was not without its problems, and, benefitting no doubt from the knowledge of men and affairs he had acquired in his active earlier years, Ṭahmāsp was able to maintain control of his realm without great difficulty. One is reminded of his contemporary Philip II of Spain administering his Empire from the little bedroom in the Escorial. And, in spite of financial difficulties caused by his meanness and signs of an increase in corruption, the contemporary observers agree that the Shah retained the devotion of his subjects. The reverence for the Shah current among the early Qizilbash, and noted by Membré as well as others, was apparently not greatly, if at all, diminished. As for the Qizilbāsh themselves, if life, particularly life at court, had changed in many ways since the beginning of the reign and even though Ṭahmāsp may have made some moves to try to limit their power, at his death in 1576 they still held practically all provincial governorships and positions of military command, as well as most of the greatest offices at court.

* * *

In September 1540 Membré left the Royal camp at Takht-i Sulaimān and, in the company of the two Muslim Arabs who had entered his service, set out for Hormuz on the Persian Gulf. The party travelled fast most of the time and

Membré's observations, though not without interest, are brief. In Isfahan he was unwell but after twenty five days he recovered and pressed on. Hormuz was reached in November. There, as already mentioned, he claimed that he passed himself off as accredited from the Emperor as well as Venice in order to persuade the Portuguese Captain that he should be helped to reach India and there catch the return fleet to Portugal.

The voyage from Hormuz to India and Membré's stay there are again treated briefly. He did not stop anywhere for long and may still not have been in the best of health. He is confused about the towns that he passed on the west coast of India. He has some observations to make, but often they are rather standard treatments of well-known curiosities, for instance, the elephant and the coconut palm. The *Relazione* ends with the sea journey to Portugal, quite briefly told, but with the horror of a bad voyage and the near death of the narrator to provide a marvellously dramatic conclusion. Storms near the Cape led to delay, which in turn led to shortage of provisions and scurvy resulting in the deaths of well over half of the four hundred on board. Membré himself was suffering a severe case of scurvy and vividly describes how he was landed at the Azores on the point of death. Yet, even *in extremis*, he was up to something: some jewels, which a Venetian jeweller of Cochin, already an acquaintance from Damascus, had asked him to deliver to Lisbon, were found among his possessions, or rather those of the unsuspecting Moors on whom he had planted them, and seized as contraband. Vitamin C no doubt had its usual effect on his scurvy and after twenty days the ship took him on to Lisbon, which was reached on 19 August 1541.

On reaching Lisbon Membré did not hurry on to Venice, but remained at the Portuguese capital. The main reason for the delay was his determination to recover the jewels which had been taken from him at Terçeira. He asked for letters to be written to the King of Portugal on his behalf, and after further delay a letter to the King and the sum of 50 ducats were sent off to him from Venice by courier. Before they arrived he had, however, decided to move on. On 26 January 1542 he met the courier on the road to Spain. What happened to the jewels in the end remains unknown, but Membré still had diplomatic business to conduct. On 2 February he was received by Charles V at Valladolid. No doubt the Emperor was interested to hear his account of the mission, which, whatever the precise terms of Membré's commission, had represented the interests of all the partners in the Holy League and not Venice alone. However, according to one of Membré's letters he went so far as to propose that Membré should set out once again for the Sophy's court, this time in his name. Remarkably, Membré states that he was about to accept this proposition but his Arab servant, terrified at the prospect of being made a slave in Persia, told the whole truth, by which we are presumably to understand that he revealed that the letters Membré claimed to have brought from Ṭahmāsp to the Emperor were not genuine. The episode needs to be considered together with the conflicting accounts of Membré's departure from the Persian court which have been discussed above. It remains a puzzle. Given permission to leave, Membré proceeded, still in secret, via Avignon, Marseilles and Genoa and reached Venice in May. On arrival he knew no one: for all we know this was his first sight of the city. He succeeded in finding Domenigo da Mosto, the former Governor of Cyprus who had sent him on his mission, and through him was presented to the Council of Ten.

* * *

The promised pension of 50 ducats a year was soon forthcoming. In addition, in fulfilling that ambition of his to serve the Signory, Membré had brought himself and his talents to its attention. Late in 1543 he was made secretary to the Ambassador sent to congratulate Sulṭān Sulaimān on his victories in Hungary, and after the mission was over he was suitably rewarded. Progressing further, in 1550 he was appointed official Dragoman to the Signory, a position which not only involved translation, interpretation and other quasi-diplomatic duties, but also the task, as well no doubt as the fees and perquisites, of overseeing commercial transactions between individual Venetian and Turkish merchants.

In the intellectual world of Venice, much interested in new developments in geography and cartography, Membré also played his part. He assisted Gianbattista Ramusio, the predecessor of our Richard Hakluyt, by collecting material for the former's great collection of Voyages from Persian merchants. He was also involved in at least two projects to produce maps. The best attested of these, an enterprise undertaken by Marc' Antonio Giustinian, in 1568, was a plan to publish a world map with captions and accompanying text in Turkish. Evidently the aim, whether realistic or not, was to appeal to a Muslim, and particularly a Turkish, market and to add to its appeal on the map itself it was stated that it had been produced by a learned Muslim of Tunis, Ḥājjī Aḥmad. Permission to publish the map seems to have been withdrawn, probably for reasons of national security, for the wooden blocks for it were for a long time in the archives of the Council of Ten. (Surviving copies come from a set printed from the blocks in 1795. At that time they were transferred to the Library of St. Mark, where, now in wormeaten condition, they still survive.) Ménage has shown that the inscriptions, with the inept spelling and incorrect grammar already referred to, are the work of a European, evidently Membré. Writing at a time when the *Relazione* was not available, Ménage was inclined to see Ḥājjī Aḥmad as a wholly fictional character, but as Scarcia points out, it is tempting to identify him with none other than the Moor from Tunis who appears accompanying Membré on his departure from the Persian court. However, if Ḥājjī Aḥmad contributed more than his name to the map, his claims to any great learning can safely be dismissed. The insight into Membré's character provided by the *Relazione* makes it clear that a fraudulent enterprise such as that of the map is quite in keeping.

When Membré retired from the post of Dragoman does not appear to be recorded. He lived to an advanced age, dying at Venice in his eighty-sixth year late in November 1595. Two wills survive from shortly before this. From the details given by Scarcia, it seems that, though he complains of having been robbed by a nephew, he was in comfortable circumstances. He had outlived Shāh Ṭahmāsp, who, after an exceptionally long reign, had died in 1576. He had outlived all his grand Qizilbāsh friends at the Persian court. The Qizilbāsh as a social group had long retained much of their power but by 1595 the reign of Shāh ʻAbbās the Great and the reforms by which he ended their dominance were well under way.

* * *

Much of the narrative of the *Relazione* is straightforward but it contains technical and obsolete vocabulary which demands to be translated by English equivalents which will be obscure to most people. In addition, many words from Turkish, Persian and other languages are used, sometimes without explanation. A glossary of terms has accordingly been provided. Biographical notes on the people mentioned by Membré are also given, where they are identifiable. Annotation to the text itself has been supplied sparingly, and precise references to sources are almost never given. The intention has been to enable the reader to follow and appreciate the story, without encumbering the book with scholarly apparatus. The bibliography contains the sources for practically all the statements in the various notes.

* * *

In concluding this introduction, it is a pleasure to express gratitude to a number of people who have assisted this work to its conclusion. Professor Angelo Piemontese kindly read through an early draft of the translation, and pointed out a number of errors. Professor Adriano Rossi and Professor Rahim Reza of the Istituto Universitario Orientale of Naples, which published the Italian text of Membré, have provided much encouragement and assistance. Among others who gave help, support and advice, Dr. Stefano Carboni, Mr. Simon Digby, Professor T. O. Gandjeï, Dr. Colin Heywood, Mr. Rüdiger Klein, Dr. D.O. Morgan and Professor J.M. Rogers deserve particular thanks. The figure on page 26 is taken from a negative supplied by the Photographic Section of the Archivio di Stato, Venice, and is published with the permission of the Archivio di Stato (Autorizzazione N. 37/1992). I am most grateful to Mr. Paul Fox for his print of the negative and also to Mrs. Catherine Lawrence for drawing the map showing Membré's route. It remains to thank the School of Oriental and African Studies for accepting the work for publication.

A.H. Morton.

Map illustrating Membré's route from Cyprus to Hormuz

R. Rioni
Kutaisi
Gori
Tiflis
GEORGIA
Zagem
SHAKKI
Lori
SHIRVAN
Erevan
CASPIAN SEA
Nakhjavan
Khuy
Van
Marand
Ardabil
Tabriz
Ujan
Maragha
Takht-i Sulaiman
GILAN
MAZANDARAN
Zanjan
Sultaniyya
Abhar
Qazvin
Varamin
KHURASAN
Qum
Kashan
PERSIA
Baghdad
Isfahan
Yazd
Basra
Shiraz
PERSIAN GULF
Lar
Bandar Hormuz
Hormuz
Muscat

ADDENDA AND CORRIGENDA TO THE FIRST EDITION

Two lines repeated in error in the first edition at the top of p. 44 have been deleted in the text of the reprint. One entry in the bibliography has been updated. In a handful of places spelling, punctuation and diacritical marks have been corrected. Half a dozen page references have been added to the index. For technical reasons it has proved impossible to preserve the precise pagination of the original. However, in the introduction and text the discrepancies arising are almost never more than half a line long, and it has not proved necessary to alter any page reference in the original index, except in two cases (pp. xvii-xviii, pp. 13-14) where the two parts of a name have come to stand either side of the page break. Both pages are now given in the index of the reprint under the relevant entries.

p. xi. It is here incorrectly stated that the Persian language is never mentioned in the *Relazione*. While no reference is made to its use during Membré's stay at Court, he does say that it was current in Lar (p. 47) and spoken by the King of Hormuz (p. 54).

pp. 41, 46, 80. Soprasi; Soprassi. The late Professor Jean Aubin expressed the opinion that a name is not intended in either case and that the text should be understood as standard Italian '*sopra si*'. This interpretation is surely correct. The Lord of Gilan is described as being *signor sopra si*, that is, lord over himself, and the King of Lar similarly as *re sopra si*, king over himself. It is their status as independent, or, more precisely, semi-independent, rulers to which attention is being drawn.

p. 50. Farnando Lintu. Professor Aubin, without going into detail, indicated that the name must stand for Fernão de Lima. Lintu is not a Portuguese name and the passage of Correa (iv, pp. 165-6) referred to in the Introduction (p. xx) states that it was a certain Fernão de Lima who brought the envoys to India in his ship.

p. 70. Chirkīn ('Filthy') Ḥasan. Dr Oric Basirov has drawn attention to the fact that originally Persian word *chirkīn*, normally meaning 'filthy' or 'grubby' in Persian, in Turkish came to mean 'ugly'. It was presumably intended in the latter sense in this case.

RELATION

PRESENTED ON THE 5 JULY 1542 BY THE PERSONAL HAND OF MICAEL MEMBRÉ RETURNED FROM THE LORD SOPHY OF PERSIA

Chapter I

From Cyprus to Turkey.

In order that Your Most Illustrious Lordships, and the Most Excellent Lords, may be informed with greater particularity of the voyage made by Your Lordships' most faithful servant, myself, Micael Membré of the isle of Cyprus, and of the zeal and desire I have ever had for their service, even though I notified them in brief of the whole from the city of Lisbon, to complete the rest of my journey to the most potent Sophy, they may follow it as I have outlined it below.

* * *

In the year 1538,[1] on the 19th of February, the Magnificent Messer Domenigo da Ca Mosto, then Lieutenant in the isle of Cyprus, in the city of Nicosia, spoke with the Magnificent Messer Bernardo Benedetti of Cyprus, Lord of the manor of Peristerona in Santo Sozomeno, which he bought from the Most Illustrious Signory. He enquired from him, as the most experienced person of the said city of Nicosia, saying that he had to find a man who would be capable of carrying a letter from the Most Illustrious Signory to the Lord Sophy, in the interest of the same Most Serene Signory; he would treat him very well and he would give a good provision to whoever went. Wherefore the said Messer Bernardo promised to look and to do all that was possible. And because I, your servant as mentioned, Micael Membré, was brought up in the house of the said Magnificent Benedettis and with their sons, especially the Magnificent Messer Zanetto, on their business, and they have many times sent me to Turkey and Syria in their name, also being related to my grandmother, and most of the time I used to continually eat and sleep in their house, the said Magnificent Messer Bernardo, knowing well that I dealt with all the foreign merchants who came from those parts and with those who know their language, decided as he was talking with me one day after dining at table, the 23rd of February or the 28th 1538, if I am not mistaken, to ask me if I knew anyone of the people of that city

---

1 In accordance with Venetian custom of the period, the year is taken to begin on 1 March. In modern terms it is 1539.

who could talk Turkish and would be able to go to Ajamia[1] at a time when the Most Illustrious Signory was at war with the Turk.

I answered that he should please tell me why. And he thus began by saying that he was about to tell me a great secret, which I should not tell to anyone in the world because there was danger there for his life and honour. And I promised that I would never tell anyone, and he continued, 'His Magnificence the Lieutenant has requested me, in the interest of our Most Illustrious Signory, that I should succeed in finding a man who would be capable of carrying a letter to the Lord Sophy, which is of the greatest importance for the Most Excellent Signory.'

So therefore the said Messer Bernardo requested that I should use my diligence to find or think of someone who would be good for that task. I, true servant of your Most Excellent Lordships, who day and night was wishing for nothing other than to spend myself for them in such service to them in order to obtain their favour, having heard the said words, replied to him, saying, 'The Lord God has sent a task of this kind to fulfil the ambition I have, which I have been waiting to achieve for a long time now. I, then, have sufficient resolution, with the help of the Lord God, to carry the said letter to the said Sophy.'

When the said Messer Bernardo heard this he judged it to be in jest and began to laugh at me, and when he saw that what I was saying was in earnest he thought he should dissuade me, saying that he would in that case suffer two afflictions, the one that he would deprive himself of me, the other that it would be he who would be the cause of my death; wherefore he was most unhappy to have told me such a thing. Finally, when his Magnificence saw that I was pressing about the matter, telling him that if he did not himself go to the Magnificent Messer Domenigo da Mosto to inform him and tell him my mind, I myself would go there to ask for such a task, he decided he should go to the said Magnificent Lieutenant and tell him of the matter, and of my resolution.

In this way the Magnificent Messer Domenigo had me called and wished to speak to me, and to see the eagerness which he had found I had. He was most greatly pleased to hear of it, and asked me which road I intended to take; to which I answered that to be able to go safely I could go from no other place than the isle of Scio,[2] that is, go first to Candy,[3] then to Scio, and from there cross Anatolia by land and go to the Sophy; in that way I would make a safe journey. When he heard this His Magnificence approved, and then he asked me where would be a good place to carry the letter, so that it would go safely and in good condition. I said he should put it in one of the board covers of a Greek book, a psalter, which was bound with boards, one on each side. In one

---

1 Persia, from Arabic *'ajam*, barbarian, Persian.

2 Chios.

3 Crete, and also its chief city, modern Heraklion/Iraklion.

of the sides it would be possible to put the letter, backed with a thin board, and make it of the same appearance as the other board, which would be of solid wood, then covering the whole with leather; in this way it would go safely. His Magnificence showed great pleasure at hearing this and questioned me about terms. To which, telling him that, putting into such manifest danger, as would be the case, life, than which there was nothing else dearer to men, and which, when lost, could not be bought again for any price, it seemed to me not to deserve less than a pension of two hundred ducats per annum. On his telling me that he had orders from the Most Illustrious Signory to spend no more than fifty ducats per annum by way of a pension, I replied that it was very well known how much I made each year in that land, which was more than a hundred and fifty ducats, living at ease in my own country and with my friends, but that I did not wish to fail in my duty, in order that the Most Illustrious Signory should know of my fidelity and the desire that I have to win its favour and to be known to it as a faithful servant. So, in order to fulfil this most fervent ambition of mine, it seemed to me that I should leave it for the said Magnificent Messer Domenico to do what he thought good. And he gave me the grant for the fifty ducats a year only.

So, when that was done, I took an old Greek book, which was a psalter, and gave it into the hands of his Magnificence, so that he could put the letter in it and cunningly make it like the other board with his own hands. His Magnificence fashioned it so well that it was not possible to know where the letter to the Lord Sophy was. Thus he gave me the book, which is still in my possession to this day. At once, through the said Magnificent Messer Bernardo Benedetti, I secretly had all my clothes and goods sold by auction, and I had too from his son Messer Zanetto twenty five ducats against my creditors[1] to that amount, which I left him to collect. And in order that no one should know of my journey, I said to my relations that I was going with corn to Candy. And the Magnificent Messer Domenico gave me the permit so that I could load. Thus, having of my own altogether three hundred and fifty ducats, with almost half I bought corn, and, of the rest, part I spent on clothes to disguise myself in the Turkish fashion and part I kept on me. Wherefore all thought that I was going to sell corn in Candy, because at that time there was a great dearth in that island.

So, on the first of March 1539, I set off from Nicosia and went to Salines[2] where there was a ship, master Stefano Pastrovicchio, loaded with corn and biscuit from Napoli de Romania;[3] in which ship I loaded the corn bought at Larnaca from Messer Pietro Martinengo, and we set out for Candy. We were at sea for 16 or 18 days, if I am not mistaken, and suddenly arrived at the said

1 *sic.*

2 Meaning the Salt-pans; the name of the port of the city of Larnaca.

3 Navplion, on the east coast of the Peloponnese.

island of Candy. I went at once to the Magnificent Duke, who, if I remember well, was called ..., and his servitors informed him that I wished to speak to him in private. His Magnificence had me called to his chamber, where a young man was present, and said to me, 'Do not be worried, for it is my son.' I requested him to be so kind to me as to make him go out, because I wished to speak with His Magnificence alone on a matter of importance. So the young man left and I gave him the letters in which the Magnificent Messer Domenico wrote to him saying that, when I needed help, he should extend all favour to me to pass on to Scio. His Magnificence, after taking and reading the letter, in his kindness treated me well, and I asked him to agree to buy the corn which I had, according to what it was worth, so that I could realize my money and go my way without losing time. Thus His Magnificence proposed that I should go then to dine and that he would have the money given to me. I at once left His Magnificence, disguised in those clothes, like the Greeks who dwell in the lands of the Turk, the beard shaved, with a Greek cap and with the shirt outside the stockings, as they wear them in Greece. So, after that day had passed, the next day I went to His Magnificence for the money, as he had promised me.

He replied that he was unable to do it because it would be necessary that all his other partners should know of it, as well as stewards and chamberlains, and that he suspected that something might therefore come to pass. Wherefore I asked him for permission to be able to sell the said corn publicly. I received it and forthwith found the bakers of the land, sold it to them and realized my money, with a profit on what it had cost. Then I found a brigantine which was going to Scio loaded with kerseys. The supercargo was a young Venetian called Marco Antonio d'Angello, whom I have seen on the Rialto just now. I asked about his home and he said that it was in Santa Trinità, in the Street of the Drasi in the house of Messer Modesto Barbetta; near San Francesco de la Vignia[1] there is a barber who knows the said young man, according to what he told me.

So I straightway spoke with the master of the said brigantine, saying that he should take me in his company to Scio, for I wanted to go to my home in Athens in Greece. He asked me my name. I said that I was called Georgio Atineo[2] son of Janin Calofrona. He said that he would willingly take me, but that I must speak with the supercargo himself. He too, when I had requested him to take me, agreed but said that I had to obtain a passport from the Admiral, because it was not possible for anyone to leave without a passport; and that it seemed to him that, because I was a subject of the Turk, he would not allow me to pass. I begged him much to help me by saying to the said Admiral that I was a man of Scio and that he knew me, and he promised to do

1 A church in the northeastern part of Venice, not far from the Arsenal. The parish of Santa Trinità (S. Ternità) was nearby.

2 Atineo meaning Athenian.

so. But because there was a man of Scio called Georgio Magnendi going in the said brigantine, who was a young man, I was shrewd enough, by taking him many times to the tavern with me to make our repast, for him to decide to please me by making the relations he had in Candy urge my case too and come with me [sc. to the Admiral], so that they made me out a passport as a man of Scio.

So, in that same month of March I set forth in the said brigantine in company with the two young men, one from Scio and the other the Venetian supercargo. We went to Santo Herini,[1] which is close to the sea: and on the top of a hill, there are houses, about 60 or 80 in number, which houses are very small. The women work linen cloth and speak Greek. And at night they keep vigil, that is, watch for the Turkish foists. So, after 2 days, if I am not mistaken, we went to the island of Nixia,[2] where we stayed 2 more days in the city itself. Now, the said city is beside the sea; and the people are Greek. The women wear a kind of very short clothing, to about the knee, and the busts of the garment are excessively low. And the master of the said brigantine was from Nixia, and because we were anxious about the Turkish foists he had wanted to land at the said island to hear what news there was. So, after that we travelled on to the isle of Scio and when we reached the said island, at the first land we touched, in company with the said Giorgi of Scio, we jumped to land, because of our anxiety about the foists; for all around the said island stand towers built of stone and in the said towers they keep watch for the said foists. Thus, at one of the towers we were told that the succeeding day, that is the days that had passed,[3] four foists passed the place. Therefore, for fear of them we went by land, both of us running to the city, which might have been 2 leagues distant. The said young man of Scio had me to lodge in his home, where there was a brother of his called Papà Sidero Magnenti, in the district of Aplottaria, beside St. George of the Greek nuns.

So, the said Father[4] greeted me with good cheer and during the night of that same day the brigantine too arrived safely. The said priest asked me my name, and I told him I was called Giorgi Calofrona of Athens. And that was because I had had many dealings with Athenian merchants, among other kinds of dealings. I used to have a young Athenian compeer, living in Cyprus, in the city of Nicosia, who is called Micali Sartor, and he always used to talk to me about his country and his home. Thus he told me that he had a brother, whose name was Giorgi, 10 years old. And he departed and they have never heard anything of him. And that was about 20 years before. I carefully took over all

---

1 Santorini or Thera.

2 Naxos.

3 *sic.*

4 Giorgi's brother was a priest, Greek *papas*.

his relationships, and his homes and everything else that was necessary, and put myself in place of his brother Giorgi; for he had been 10 years old and it was 20 more that he had been missing from his home, which would come to be my own age, that is, 30. So for that reason I had called myself Giorgi Calofrona - for his family was Calofrona - so that if any Athenian happened to have questioned me I would know everything to say. So, with the grace of My Lord God, in that way I always went in safety, as I have talked with many Athenian merchants who have kept me good company, and they all believed in me.

So I stayed about 10 days in the said city of Scio and in that time, with great diligence, I made friendships with the Christian merchants who used to come from that part of Anatolia, that is from a city called Vurulla[1] and because I frequently used to lead the said merchants to the tavern, at my expense, they had become willing to keep me company. Wherefore, we bought some henna, sacks 14 in number, which was from the Turkish prizes taken in Candy. Therefore the people of Candy were sending the said henna to Scio and selling it there. So we found a boat and had the said henna loaded; and together with other Turkish merchants we came to the land of Anatolia, that is to a place called Cheshme.[2]

1 Modern Turkish Urlu. A small town between Cheshme and Smyrna (Izmir).

2 Modern Turkish spelling Çeşme, on the mainland in the Straits of Chios, opposite the island.

Chapter II

Anatolia. The Crimea. Georgia.

That was in the month of April 1539. In that place there is an inn, called *caravansarai*, and on the left, beside the said caravanserai, stands a stone fortress above on a hill, and in the said fortress are janissaries, about 50 in number. The next day we took pack-mules and loaded the said henna and went to a town called Vurulla, where the houses of the said Christian merchants were; on which journey we were on the road for one and 1/2 days. Then we left the said place and in company with the muleteers we went to the city of Mannisia,[1] where was living Sulṭān Muṣṭafā himself, the eldest son of the Grand Turk. And from the said place Vurulla till entering the said city we travelled for 2 days. So we lodged in a *caravansarai*, that is inn; which inn is to the east, facing the square. And to the north stands a mosque, in which mosque the said Sulṭān Muṣṭafā says his prayers every Friday. Thus, on one of those Fridays I saw the said Sulṭān Muṣṭafā go into the said mosque. So, as for his person, he is a slightly dark young man, tall, without a beard; his mustachios were beginning to go dark. In his company men on horseback, about 35 or 40 of them, go before, well dressed, and then he himself, together with his *lâla* or tutor, an old man with a white beard; and in front of him footmen, 9 in number, each one of the 9 wearing a very long and wide white shirt. And each one of them carries a bow and 50, 60 arrows, with their plumes on their heads. Thus when the mounted men, called *sipāhīs*, reach the door of the said mosque, they all go around to one side and the other and make a kind of passageway. So then the said Sulṭān Muṣṭafā passes, together with his *lâla* and his footmen, and enters the said mosque. And as he passes, the *sipāhīs* who stand on one side and the other cry, '*Allāh, Allāh. Devletlu khūndkār ömrini ẓiyade eylesin*,' that is, 'God prolong the life of his father', who has the name *Khūndkār*, and they all bow their heads until the said one passes. And after he has performed his prayers he mounts and goes into his house with those mentioned.

His house stands within a garden and the said garden is enclosed all round by an earth wall, and on the north-west stands its great gate, with the porters, that

---

1 Modern Manisa. Smyrna itself, which lay on the direct route to Manisa, seems to have been bypassed, as well as other towns later on the route through Anatolia.

is guards. And facing the gate is a square for galloping horses, wherefore it is called *maidān*, and in the middle of the said *maidān* stands a very long and tall mast of wood; and on the top of the said mast is an apple of gilded copper. For, sometimes, as they gallop their horses they shoot arrows at the said apple.[1]

Therefore, as I have said, in the said city of Manissia we sought to sell the said henna which we had in common, which we could not dispose of so soon. And when I saw that, I said to my companions that I would willingly realize the capital and something small by way of profit, because I wished to go home to my country. So my said companions gave me the capital and a small carpet and 50 aspers profit; and because the roads were very dangerous because of robbers and also in order not to give reason for anyone to have any suspicion of me, I decided to buy carded[2] cotton in the said city of Manissia, 8 sums in number, because in the city I wanted to go to there was no cotton and the merchants used to carry it from the said city of Manissia. So I decided to buy it myself too, with the intention of having the company of the *agosatti*, that is, muleteers, and in order to be recognized as a merchant. Therefore, after having bought the said cotton, I loaded it on mules and together with the muleteers and others we went to another city, called Caraissare,[3] to which we were about 8 days on the road. We travelled always over hills and mountains and a small amount of plain. The loads of cotton I put in a *caravansarai*, that is, inn, where there was a weigh-beam or great balance of wood with which they weigh all the cottons and other goods. And I lodged in another caravanserai, called Pesecan[4] where botanoes are sold. After 4 or 5 days I sold the said cotton in such a way that I lost about 6 ducats of the capital.

The said city stands at the foot of a mountain, and on the summit of the said mountain is a small stone fortress, within which janissaries are stationed. And in the city resides the Sanjaq himself, and also many Armenian Christians. And the aspers of the said city are reckoned as very bad and are worth 75 to the gold ducat. So I bought a donkey in the said city, and, in company with certain Armenian merchants and Turks, set off to go to Angora,[5] where the camlets are made. And on the road we had great fear of robbers. We passed a city called Suverrassar[6]; then we entered the said city of Angora (on the road we had been 10 days, always travelling with camels; so I lodged in a *caravansarai*, that is an

---

1 Though Membré does not say so the similar mast he describes at Tabriz was used for the same purpose. In both Turkey and Persia the mast was called *qabaq*, a Turkish word.

2 *macluso*, representing the originally Arabic word for carded, *maḥlūj*.

3 Modern Afyonkarahisar or Afyon.

4 *-can* stands for *han* (< Persian *khān*), meaning caravanserai, but the rest of the name is uncertain.

5 Ankara. Anguri in the text.

6 Sivrihisar.

inn, which is called Cursci can.[1]), a great city with many gardens all around. Which city has a stone fortress next to the city on the north. And a mile outside the city, passing a certain river, stands a monastery of Armenians, which monastery is called San Petro, if I remember well.[2] In the monastery is the grave of a Frenchman who was killed in the said city of Angora on his return from India, because he had many precious jewels, according to what the said Armenians told me.[3] And outside the monastery are many marble sepulchres, with the name of each one of the dead written on them, part in Greek letters, part in Latin.

So then I set off from the said city of Angora in the company of other Turkish merchants to go to another city, called Cancria;[4] and I bought camlets and mohairs to the number of 25, which I loaded on one of the muleteers' mules, and I myself rode on my donkey. On the road we travelled about 5 days; then we entered the said city of Cancria, and I lodged in a *caravansarai*, that is, inn. The chambers of the said inn were for the most part built of boards of wood, and outside the door there was a smith for horses, and opposite, or to the west, stood a tavern where wine was sold. The said city is small and stands on level ground next to certain gardens.

Then there came a caravan to the said city from the direction of Arzinjan,[5] the frontier of Ajamia. There were many Turkish and Armenian merchants in the caravan, who were going to Constantinople with silk goods. From the said people I heard how they were not allowing any caravan to pass into Ajamia. So, too, all those who came from those parts of Ajamia, the Ottomans took their merchandise as contraband. And of all those who found themselves on that frontier, both merchants and poor strangers, they had demanded sureties; and all those who had no sureties to give, they put in prison. Thus those lands were in the greatest confusion. And they had also made a proclamation to all those who found themselves on the roads to go to Ajamia without the Signor's licence: whoever should be taken should have his head cut off, and whoever cut it off should have his property. Therefore, having heard such things, I decided that it would not be possible to pass by the said ways. But the Lord God, who is just, immediately lit up for me another most safe road, by way of the Mar Maggior.[6]

---

1 Possibly, as the editors suggest, the Qūrshūnlū (Kurşunlu) Han is intended. The fifteenth-century building and the adjacent bazaar now serve as a museum. Qūrshūnlū means 'leaden', and presumably in such cases implies that the building is roofed with lead.

2 Later accounts say the monastery was named after the Virgin Mary.

3 The French jewel-merchant must be the one the story of whose death was heard by António Tenreiro in Aleppo late in 1528. His jewels were taken by the Sultan.

4 Chankiri, in Modern Turkish Çankırı.

5 Modern Turkish Erzincan. Arzincan in the text.

6 The Black Sea.

So I departed from the said city of Cancria and went to another city called Namisso,[1] which stands by the Mar Maggior. And on the road we passed another city called Marzivan,[2] a city with many gardens all around; and we were on the road days 4 in number, if I am not mistaken. For two days we travelled on a good road and for two more, in the vicinity of the said Mar Maggior, we travelled through many mountains full of trees, woods and many waters. In the said city of Namisso I lodged in a *caravansarai*, that is, inn, of stone, which stands very close to the shore where the ships are loaded. And half the houses of that city are of wood. At the gate of the said caravanserai is a smith who shoes the horses. And on that street stands the square, with shops on one side and the other; and there is a fortress of stone by the sea towards Trebizond.[3] The city is very small and towards the west, beside the sea, stand stores of wooden boards and taverns which sell wine, which are in the hands of the Greek Christians.

Then I found a ship ready to go to Kaffa, loaded with cotton botanoes from Adana and Tarsus. In the said ship were Turkish and Greek merchants; the sailors were Greek. So I straightway found the master of the ship and came to agreement with him; and because the sailors were Greek the master treated me kindly. And on the instant I loaded my camlets, which I had bought in Angora, and also sold that donkey of mine. And then we set out for Kaffa (If I am not mistaken, that was in the month of June 1539); and we went straight to Kaffa, remaining 18 days at sea with contrary winds and calms. The city of Kaffa consumes much cotton cloth because of the dyers. Then, together with the merchants, we lodged in a caravanserai called Cursi can.[4] And that same day I found another Greek ship loaded with salt and other merchandise, master Khoja Ra'is of Sinop, which was ready to go to Mingrelia; and the next day I straightway found the master in the company of an Athenian barber, and I spoke with him, saying that he should carry me to Mingrelia. He replied that he would do so gladly. So, on the third day I loaded those few mohairs and camlets and on the fourth day set off on the said ship; from there we always sailed in sight of land, and in 18 or 16 days we reached a place called Anaclia,[5] territory of the King Dadian of Mingrelia. In this place there is a large river, which the ships go into when they are unloaded. Then the ship stops there on the said shore and holds a market within the ship, all by barter: they give cloth and take cloth. The Mingrelians come alongside the ship in their boats and

---

1 Samsun.

2 Merzifon.

3 Text: Trapezonda.

4 The editors tentatively suggest that, as with the caravanserai at Angora, the name may stand for Qūrshūnlū Han.

5 Araclia in the text, but doubtless referring to Anaklia by the mouth of the Inguri river.

each brings a bag with his cloth. So in that way they hold their markets.

Salt is not found in the said place of Mingrelia. Leather and sheepskin and other goods are very dear. In the said place of Mingrelia there comes forth much yellow wax, linen thread and canarine silk of Zagem,[1] and they also sell many slaves. Then the next day the said ship began unloading salt and loading it into the boats to send to be sold in a market which they were going to hold in those days on the Phasis,[2] at a place called Culauropa. And I went with the said boats to the said place where the market is held; and we travelled always in the boats on a river called the Phasis for 8 days. On the said river are infinitely many trees, on one side and the other, flat country; so each night the boat stopped by land and in the morning travelled, proceeding by sail. In the said place many flies and mosquitoes are found, which I surely could not have survived if I had not covered my face with a cloth, and all my body and hands; for the said mosquitoes were of such a kind that, when they had found uncovered flesh, they treated it so that the blood flowed as if a phlebotomy had been performed. The Mingrelians go very poorly dressed, all with short cotton clothes and unshod, which we value for 0. But it is quite true that all their feet look as if they were scabby. They wear on their heads a piece of felt like a mitre; but they are very small. To the north are many high mountains. The Mingrelian gentlemen wear very long clothes and a pair of boots of sheepskin leather, not having a leather sole but all of that sheepskin; also coloured felt on the head; and they are unbearded, with long moustaches such as the Iberians[3] have.

So, because of the mosquitoes, as I have said, we endured great trouble till arriving at the said place of the market, called Culauropa. The said place is by the river called Phasis, to the south-east. It is on a plain within a wood and the houses are of wood, about 50 in number; and in the said place most of the households are Jews; which Jews buy slaves of the Mingrelian nation and make them Jews; and in this the Mingrelians do not say them nay. And in the middle of the square where the market assembles stands a Church, of Saint George, its vault of copper, with two little bell-towers. The Iberians celebrate the mass, and outside the church stands a wooden mast with three or four of their daggers [...] and two swords all stuck into the said wood. So, in that said place Culauropa I found a man from Scio called Zane, who was married there with an old lady of Mingrelia. Wherefore he made me alight at his house. I also found another, who was a Venetian, married to a Mingrelian. His name was Bernardo

---

1 A town in the south of Kakhetian Georgia, long abandoned.

2 The Classical name of the famous river in Colchis, where the Golden Fleece was kept. Now called the Rioni.

3 Georgians. The Mingrelians were themselves Georgians.

Moliner,[1] a man of 45, who told me that he had been a miller in Venice and that in that place in Mingrelia he had children, 3 in number, two male, and a female married to one of the Mingrelians.

Now, many poor people come to the said market, and other Iberian merchants with silks, which they exchange, cloth for cloth, without other money being used. And the said fair lasts days 3 in number, and then all depart. There only remain those families of the Jews and 10 or 12 families of Mingrelians. So after the said fair was ended, as I have said, I set off in the company of a Greek merchant, Calojero of Trebizond by name, and we crossed the said river Phasis in a boat and went to a city of Iberia called Kutaisi, of King Bāshī āchuq. We were on the road 2 1/2 days, always travelling over level ground with many gardens. Then we entered the city called Kutaisi, crossing a river by a wooden bridge. Which river passes beside the said city; and to the north stands a stone fortress on a hill, in which there is a church; and on the other side, to the south east, is a meadow where the said King runs his horses. And beside the river he was building some houses of stone with many vaults, which they said were for the King. However, most of the houses in the said city are of wood for the most part and there are many gardens.

I lodged in the house of some goldsmiths from Trebizond, who kept me good company, and together with the said Calogero. In the said city cloth pays 5 per bale in tax. The coins of the said city are like Turkish aspers, and they are called *tanka.* The stamp on them is some Iberian letters. The King can have, by what was said, horsemen 7,000 in number, who are called *aznāvurs*. The said *aznāvurs* are much bigger men than the rest of us and have long, black moustaches; and they shave the beard. And they wear clothes, that is very long stockings of cotton cloth, of very coarse cotton, and cloth breeches, with, over the stockings, boots of sheepskin leather, and a quilted[2] shirt of coarse cotton cloth, and a very long dolman of cotton cloth; and on the head a felt hat with a very long fine top. Which felts are coloured. Their arms are swords, lances, shield, bow and arrows, iron mace, mail coat, cuirassine, half helmet, plate gauntlets, good horses with good silk covers such that an arrow cannot go through them. So, when one of the said *aznāvurs* rides to go to the field of battle, he wears all those arms. The said city of Kutaisi is very small.

After 7 or 8 days we went our way to another city called Gori, on which we were 4 days on the road, travelling always over very high mountains full of woods and with many waters, on which roads there is much mire; and about a day from the said city of Gori we passed by a fortress which stood on the summit of a mountain, and was in ruins for the most part. Then we came to a

---

1 Moliner means miller.

2 The translation assumes that the *pottido* of the text is connected with Italian *inbottire*, to stuff, quilt, rather than Hindi *paṭṭī* or Persian *pāytāba* as suggested by the editors.

place where there were houses to the number of about 70, all Jews, and beside that place passed a sweet stream, like a canal. Thus, a river passes by the city called Gori. And with the horses we passed the said river and entered the city and lodged in the house of some Trapezuntines. The city is half of houses of wood and the other half of earth and part of stone. Which city is small and to the north stands a stone fortress, partly in ruins. The King of the said place is called King Luarsab; he has horsemen called *aznāvurs*, c. 5,000 in number, by the account of his gentlemen. The people who live in the said city are half Armenians and the other half Iberians. They do not have salt, save that which comes from the lands of the Sophy. Then, having loaded the mules, after 8 days I departed and went to another city called Tiflis, in the company of an Armenian of Lori. Which city belongs to the said King Luarsap; to it we travelled 1 1/2 days. The said city of Tiflis is very large but the greater part of it was destroyed on account of the many wars the said Iberians have made among themselves.

Chapter III

Persia. The Royal Camp, The Court of Shāh Ṭahmāsp. Membré's Audience with the Shah.

So the next day we departed, in company with five other Armenians who were going to Lori,[1] the first of the Sophy's cities, which borders on Iberia. From there [Tiflis] we travelled always south-east, or south, for days about 7 in number, by a road with many robbers and many mountains and hills covered with forests. The said King Luarsab pays 1,000 ducats tribute to the Sophy each year. The city of Lori is a fortress of stone and beside the said fortress, on the north, a river passes from west to east; and all around that city are villages, all Armenians, some of whom obey the Sophy and some the King of Iberia, that is King Luarsab. Now, as soon as I arrived in the said fortress of Lori, I presented myself before the Captain of the said fortress, who was named Muḥammad Khalīfa, the son of Shāh 'Alī Sulṭān Chapnī, and begged him for help, so that he should send me as quickly as possible to his Lord, the Sophy, which could produce results of great importance. When the said Captain heard this he at once ordered 7 men to accompany me to the Sophy's court and gave me a horse to ride because my horse was very weary and could not carry me.

So that night the said Captain treated me with the greatest honour and favour, and in the morning he sent me on my way with those I have mentioned. On the way we journeyed for about 3 days, always over very high mountains covered with forests; then we entered another road, all through hills, for about 2 days; then we journeyed over plains all the time for 4 more days, during which we passed on the road a city called Nakhjavān, at which time they were building certain new houses in the said city for the Sulṭān Mantashā , who is in Erevan. Then, from the said city we came to another called Marand, a very small city, with many gardens. So, throughout all that country through which we travelled, as far as the city of Marand, the villages were all Christian Armenians, subject to the Sophy.

---

1 The ruins of Lori, which occupied a naturally strong position on the Dzoraget river, are near Stepanavan in the Armenian Republic.

Then we found the Shah, at about 2 leagues beyond the said city of Marand, lodging in the meadows with his *urdū*, that is, the army with its tents. So, the said men who were in my company took me to the dwelling of Shāh 'Alī Sulṭān, the father of the said Muḥammad Khalīfa, the Captain of Lori. When he had seen me, the said Shāh 'Alī Sulṭān was greatly pleased and much overjoyed. He at once mounted and went to the court of the said Shāh Ṭahmāsp Sophy, to inform him of my coming. When the Sophy heard the news he was greatly pleased and replied to the said Shāh 'Alī Sulṭān that he must keep me for 3 days, and then introduce me to his presence, together with the Most Illustrious Signory's letter, and treat me well, for such is his custom. That was in the month of August, 1539.

The next day, there were come from Anatolia, that is from the province of Arzinjan, Turcomans of 'Alī,[1] with their families and animals, about 800 households in number, who had come for the Shah's sake. Thus, there were of those Turcomans, horsemen, with their arms and lances, to the number of 600, who were stationed over against the court of the said Sophy, at a distance, riding round and round; all together they kept crying, '*Allāh, Allāh*'. That was in the morning, the day after I reached the Sophy's court. So, as I have just said, the said Turcomans of 'Alī, on horseback, were crying, '*Allāh, Allāh*', until the Shah came forth from his apartments, at the entrance. Then he ordered the greatest of their chiefs to be summoned, and, one by one, they came and kissed the foot of the said Shah. Thus they all came. The Shah gave each one cloth for clothing and his cap, which they call *tāj*. Then the said Turcomans gave presents to the Shah, each, according to his means, so many animals: some gave horses, some wethers and some camels. Then the Shah ordered them to three parts of his lands, that is, he sent one part to the province of Khurasan, another part to the province of Shīrvān, and the other part to the province of Iraq.

The tents which the said Shāh Ṭahmāsp had in his company were many: according to what I was able to count with my own eyes, he seemed to have 5,000. Of his horsemen, as it seemed to me, he had 14,000 in number, without the servants. Of horses and mules he had so many that they could not be counted. All the plains were full of animals.

So, as I have indicated, when the third day had passed, in accordance with the Shah's order, the said Shāh 'Alī Sulṭān had me presented before the said Sophy and I delivered the Most Illustrious Signory's letter into the hand of the said Sophy, as I reported to Their Lordships in detail in my first letter, from the Most Excellent King of Portugal's city of Lisbon. So, then, the said Shāh Ṭahmāsp Sophy departed from the said place and went towards Marāgha, together with his *urdū*, that is, army.

---

[1] The term Turcomans of 'Alī (*de Alì*) does not seem to appear elsewhere, nor is its meaning obvious. Possibly it conceals a tribal name, Takkalū perhaps.

However, to inform your Most Excellent Lordships more particularly, the customs and ways of the court of the said Sophy are of this manner, that is, there was a cord as thick as a finger, with which was formed a complete circle, like a courtyard surrounded with a wall, and having two entrances. Every three paces there was a wooden stake on the cord; on the top of the said pole was an iron ring, through which the said cord passed; and on the end of the said pole was an iron point, which was fixed in the ground. The said poles were half a rod long. So his court was of this manner. Within the said cord were his pavilions, and in the first part, on coming through the entrance in the said cord, over against it, is the palace where he gives audience, which they call *dīvānkhāna*. This palace has three pavilions, one behind the other, and the second pavilion is very large. There, within, stands an *utāq*, which is made of sticks of gilded wood in the form of a dome and covered over with scarlet. Upon the cloth is foliage, cut out and sewn with silk. Within, on the ground there was a red felt, lined with a kind of woollen canvas, and over the said felt there were very fine carpets of silk, on which appeared figures of many animals and foliage. In the third of the tents in the audience palace he sleeps when it is not cold. And after the third tent is his privy, of a kind of cloth with sticks, which form a long room. So his court was like this.

The first pavilion is meant when he gives audience, seated with his vassals; on the four sides of the said first pavilion the Sulṭāns, the most honoured of them, sit all in a row; behind these Sulṭāns, at a little distance, sit other Sulṭāns, of low rank; behind these Sulṭāns sit the *qūrchīs* or cavalrymen, row upon row; in such a way that the place of audience is all surrounded by men sitting on the ground. Those who are most honoured have a large parasol, that is shade, which is called *sāyabān*, with which he keeps off the sun. The others are seated on the ground all day until the King goes into his apartments. In his company, acting as porters without the pavilion, stand those they call *yasāvuls*, with sticks two cubits and more long, with the end of silver and with a little gilt or coloured knob; they are only of a finger's thickness.

Among all these are six or seven, whom I know, who stand closer to the King than the other porters, those who stand outside at the entrance of the pavilion; and when the Shah wishes to speak with someone they go to call him to come within and speak. Therefore these six or seven men are called *Muṣāḥib*, that is beloved and friend of the King. They are these: Qarā Khalīfa Shāmlū, which Qarā Khalīfa is a man with a black beard, neither very fair nor very dark; he rides well, is valiant, and the King regards him with great favour. The said Qarā Khalīfa has two brothers who are in the service of Bahrām Mīrzā, the brother of the Shah. One of the brothers of the said Qarā Khalīfa wears an arrow upon his turban-cloth, and is Bahrām Mīrzā's *Yasāqī*; the other is his *Qūrchī*. The said Qarā Khalīfa has two wives, one from Tabriz, the other from Shīrvān. By the one from Tabriz he has two sons and a daughter, whom he has married to the son of a *qūrchī* and *yasāvul*; one son, a youth of 19 years is called Aḥmad and the Shah has made him his *qūrchī*. The other son, Han Mocassal, is little and is learning his letters. By the wife from Shīrvān he also has another son, a year old at that time. The said Qarā Khalīfa previously took another wife also and has left her; by her too he has a son, 7 years old at that time. So his dwelling is in the *maidān* in Tabriz, that is, in the square, near where *bughrā* is sold. Near the said *bughrā* there is a gateway which leads to a narrow street, leading west, and opposite, near his dwelling is a *qūrchī*, called Ḥusain Ibrāhīm Āqā [?]. So, in the courtyard of his dwelling, as one enters by the gate, there is the palace where he gives audience, and behind the palace is the kitchen; after the kitchen there is a wall which runs with a *caravansarai* or inn, and on the left are the stables for the horses. The courtyard is small, and has a little garden, and on the other side is the chamber in which he sleeps at midday.

As I have said, these *yasāvuls* stand in the palace of audience. Then, 30 or 25 paces behind those pavilions of the palace are the chambers in which he sleeps, which chambers have the like, only in addition there is the stew, that is bath, which is a dome, one of those I mentioned above. But it is quite true that the covering of the said dome is of white felt, sometimes half red. So, outside the entrance stand the porters, old men, about five of them.[1] To the west is another dome, covered with scarlet, as I have described it above, in which are painters. And outside the King's court is his kitchen, and from there the other tents of his supplies; and next stand the tents of the most beloved of the Lords, that is Bahrām Mīrzā his brother and Sām Mīrzā his brother, the Sayyids of Uskū and others, after a pavilion. In such a way that there were tents as far as a man could see, all well-ordered, with their streets. In the court, when the King sits, all sit; when he stands up all those of the court stand up. In the morning, when he goes forth from his chamber to go to the place of audience, he has two men, each of whom carries a steel drum in his hand and begins to cry out, praising God and cursing 'Umar, 'Uthmān and Abū Bakr, and says, '*Ṣad hazār la'nat bar 'Umar, 'Uthmān, Abū Bakr*', and goes behind crying out until the King comes to sit. Then they fall silent. And when he wishes to return to his chamber they cry out in the same way until he enters the chamber. His brother likewise, when he wishes to go to the palace, has one of these people, called *tabarrā'īs*, who cries out the same until he comes to sit down. Also there are the Sayyids of Uskū, and Qāḍī-yi Jahān, his Minister and Khalīfa, and Shāh qulī Khalīfa, the Muhrdār, that is, he who seals the King's affairs. This Muhrdār is a rather fat man, with a slight defect in his eye and a short beard. He has a son who is the Shah's *parvānachī*. His dwelling in Tabriz is to the

---

1 Here the entrance to the women's quarters and the guardians at its entrance are presumably meant.

east, near a bath, facing the river, on the right bank; also the Qūrchībāshī, a man with a white beard, who also goes with a *tabarrā'ī* crying out before him. His dwelling in Tabriz is to the west, by a bath, and in his courtyard there is a truly beautiful garden. All these great Lords too, each one of them has one or two of those *tabarrā'īs* who curse the Ottomans.

As I have said, to return to my story, when the three days ordained by the Shah had passed, the said Shāh 'Alī Sulṭān brought me into his presence. He was then in the place of audience, with those beautiful pavilions, all decorated with cut designs of foliage inside and, on the floor carpets of great price. The King was thus seated upon a *takya-namad*, that is a felt of Khurasan, which was of great price; and beside him was his sword, with its scabbard depicted like a lion's skin,[1] and his bow and four or five arrows. On one side were seated his vassals, on the other, if I remember well, those Lords, that is, his brother Bahrām Mīrzā, the Sayyids of Uskū, Qāḍī-yi Jahān, Gūkcha Sulṭān, Shāh qulī Khalīfa and the Qūrchībāshī, and others I do not remember. As *yasāvuls*, there were Tachiatan Masur [?], Qarā Khalīfa, Sulaimān Chelebī. Tachiatan Masur is a stout man with a short beard; he would be about 36 years old. There was also another *yasāvul*, who was called Kūpik-kirān, that is 'dog-slayer'. He is a very stout and short man, with a short beard, and has a large paunch. Also another *yasāvul* who is called Kachal Shāhvirdī, and another called Farrukhzād Beg, the chief of the *yasāvuls*, stout, with a half white beard. Another is Nāranjī Sulṭān, a man with a short black beard, who is rather thin and dark, not very fair. He is a Kurd and wears orange, knows well how to play instruments and sings well. He has a son, a young man of nineteen years, called Shāh Khurram [?], who was in the service of Bahrām Mīrzā; the Shah has since taken him and made him his *parvānachī*. So the said Nāranjī Sulṭān is a *yasāvul*; he also has a sister who has a son and a daughter. Whereof the son, who is twenty years old, is called Shāh qulī Beg; he is in the service of Bahrām Mīrzā, as his *parvānachī*. The husband of the said Nāranjī Sulṭān's sister is with Mantashā Sulṭān in Erevan, and the sister lives with the said Nāranjī. So the clothes of the said Nāranjī Sulṭān are all orange; and so, too, his tents, camels, swords, stick, down to the paper he writes on, all are orange coloured. Another, who is called Ḥusain Beg, is *qūrchī muṣāḥib* of the said Shāh Ṭahmāsp. There is another with a long white beard, who is Shāh qulī. His house is towards the dwelling of the Sayyids of Uskū and he is father-in-law to Qarā Khalīfa; as for the other *yasāvuls*, I do not recollect their names. Another was Shāhvirdī Beg, *dārūgha* of the city of Tabriz.

So, in the company of the said Sulṭān Shāh 'Alī Chapnī, I entered the pavilion of the said Shah, as I have mentioned, and I made him the due

1 The text has lion, but perhaps a design striped like a tiger's skin may be meant.

reverence. I was given the command to sit, for all were seated. And for the moment he let me sit for a while and then he asked me wherefore I had come. So I replied that the Most Illustrious Signory, being most loyal and friendly, was desirous of obtaining his friendship, recognizing clearly and truly that he was true Emperor; therefore it had sent me thither to his presence with express orders and commission to deliver that letter with information most agreeable, to his benefit and to the destruction of his enemies, the Ottomans, as was explained more fully in the said letter. So, when the said Sophy understood my proposal, he was greatly pleased; and I at once showed him the book, inside which was the letter, disguised as a board; and I said that his letter was there. His brother Bahrām Mīrzā had the book given to him by Qarā Khalīfa, and asked which part the letter was in, since both the covers were of the same sort. So I showed him. The said Qarā Khalīfa drew a small knife and cut the outer leather and the board. Seeing the letter thus, well attached with glue, all were most greatly pleased and the letter was pulled out of the said book. He set about cutting open a piece of the other board of the said book, thinking that there would be another letter there, and, of course, found wood. Then he gave me the book and the letter remained with him. At this moment the Qūrchībāshī said, 'Well do they say that all nations have one eye and the Franks two.'[1]

So the said Sophy asked me the way I had travelled, for it seemed a great thing to him that I had been able to pass through and escape such dangers, especially as he had heard of the diligence which the Turk was using on the frontier to let no man pass. So I told him of my journey, at which he was much pleased. Then he asked me what man I was. I told him that I was a Venetian, and he asked me if I had a father and mother, brothers or sisters; and about my condition and what my age was. I told him that I had a father and a mother, and a brother, and that I was a Venetian gentleman, that my age was 30, as he could see from my appearance. So, when that was over, he gave me leave to go home and rest, and entrusted me to the said Shāh 'Alī Sulṭān. Then he ordered clothes to be given to me, and about eighty ducats and a horse.

---

1 Compare the remark of Uzun Ḥasan Āqquyūnlū to the earlier Venetian envoy, Barbaro, 'The world has three eyes; the Cathayans have two of them and the Franks one.'

Chapter IV

The Camp, continued. To Marāgha. Departure for Tabriz.

So then, after two or three days had passed, he departed from that place in Marand and went towards Marāgha, and I remained in the company of Shāh 'Alī Sulṭān Chapnī. The said Sulṭān is a rather stout man, 60 years old, with his beard half and more white. He has three sons; one is called Muḥammad Khalīfa and another Dede Beg; I do not remember the name of the third because he was not with his father, but at Varāmīn, where his mother is.

And when the army intends to move and go to another place, or, as they say in their tongue, *urdū*, then in the middle of the night they load the camels and mules of the King with a kind of flaming torch, which they call *ishik*, which is a stout pole of wood, three fingers thick and half a rod long; and on the top of the said pole there is a round iron plate, one palm across, and around the said iron there is a fine iron grid, half a palm high, and on top an iron ring, within which they put rags of old cloth, soaked in a certain oil which they call *naft*, which is found in a well in Shīrvān. And they light the rags of the said cloth with fire and it burns fiercely and lasts three or four hours, making a fierce blaze; so, at the end of the said wooden pole there is a piece of iron. In such a way that, when that torch is seen at night, everyone immediately loads and follows the flame; and they all go, one following the other. And at the place where the King's pavilions are pitched, they all lodge themselves according to their rank; some lodge near the court, some at a distance, according to their quality. And thus they go, one after the other. And at the beginning of the said *urdū* is the piazza with all the craftsmen and merchandise, and kitchens for food, all together with their tents.

The King's court removes at midnight, and the army travels one behind the other, like a caravan, and goes 4 or 5 leagues. As for the King's apartments, they go and put everything in the place where they are to stand and yet when the other end is loading it will be perhaps three hours of the day, while they are still loading in the first place.[1] The King has a captain for allotting quarters,

[1] The sentence is clumsy but the main point is obvious enough. It was normal for the great man on tour to carry two sets of tents. When camp was moved one set could be sent ahead and erected ready for the occupants' arrival, while the set currently in use did not have to be struck until after departure. Ṭahmāsp's third set, left at Marand, was perhaps a more elaborate one,

who knows the places where it is possible to camp and organizes the tent-pitchers; and in whatever place he orders they pitch the pavilions of the King. Thus the said King carries with him three sets of furniture for the court; that is, the one that was pitched at the said place in Marand remained there; then the camels and mules proceeded, loaded with another court of pavilions. Then the King slept until one or two hours of the day; the whole *urdū* arises and follows the King's camels. Then the Lords, with their arms, and the *qūrchīs* mount and stand outside the King's pavilion, waiting for him to come out to mount. And after he has come forth from the pavilion to mount, they sound the trumpets in the manner for battle, and those men called *tabarrā'īs*, who cry out, that is curse the Ottomans, go in front on foot crying out, and they take turns with each other crying out until he enters those other tents that have been pitched. So then they load those other tents which were left behind and they come by degrees and arrive towards evening. So, in that manner the *urdū* moves with the court.

And every day the people in the said *urdū* increase, for they come from throughout all his provinces, and those people come with their wives, children and everything. All have their own camels on which they carry flour, barley, fine fat, that is, butter, and kitchen equipment, tents, carpets, draperies and arms. And they carry everything with them and so leave their houses empty; thus, each Lord has 50 or 60 camels and 20 to 30 mules, some more, some less. But, as for the *qūrchīs*, who are the cavalry troopers, the most wretched of them has four or more camels and three or four mules and horses. So there is in the said *urdū* an infinite number of animals and servants.

When the King rides about 10 footmen go before him, who are called *shāṭirs*; each of them wears a white cloth skirt, cut short to the knees; and they wear trousers, and have plumes on their heads, and on the front of their belts, a little bell. And such men always go in company with Qāḍī-yi Jahān, his minister, the Sayyids of Uskū and the Qūrchībāshī, and sometimes his brother Bahrām Mīrzā. In front go the banners, which they call *'alam*, which are lances covered with red broadcloth, with two points, and on the top of the lance a circle, and, inside the said circle, certain letters of copper, cut out and gilded, which say, '*'Alī walī Allāh; lā ilāh illā Allāh; 'Alī walī allāh wa Allāhu Akbar.*' That is what the words say. They are carried in the hand on horseback. And all the peoples go, about 5 or 6 ... As many standards go as there are kingdoms, and below the said letters are armozeens of red silk with double points, and behind them go the footmen, then the King in company with those mentioned; then the Lords and *qūrchīs*, that is the cavalrymen, and the said *urdū* passes on.

---

which, since the court did not return to Marand this year, must at some stage have been taken back to store at Tabriz.

And when the people see it they give way for it to pass; for the *yasāvuls*, that is, officers deputed for this, go before and make way be made for the King to pass. And those who see him all bow their heads to the ground, and say, '*Shāh, Shāh*', and do reverence. And when he passes by some village, the villagers arrive, 100 or 200, with their women; and they come to meet the Shah with their instruments and sing praises of God, saying, '*Lā ilāh illā Allāh*', *id est*, 'Above God there is no other God', and perform other ceremonies of theirs together with their *khalīfa*, that is village headman and priest.[1]

After more than half of the *urdū* has gone by, the Shah's maidens pass on fine horses; and they ride like men and dress like men, except that on their heads they do not wear caps but white kerchiefs. And in the company of those maidens go 10 or 12 old men, who are called *īshīk-āqāsīs*, that is masters of the house. And I have seen that there were about 14-15 of those maidens, and they were beautiful, though their faces could not be fully seen. But what could be seen was beautiful and very fair. And sometimes they galloped and performed marvels with their horses, making them jump and do many other skilful tricks. They went thus to behind the court, where the Shah's tents were pitched.

Some of the Lords take much pleasure with falcons. In particular, the two brothers of the King, Bahrām Mīrzā and Sām have many falcons. Shāh Ṭahmāsp does not take pleasure in hunting with birds, or dogs;[2] only in going into certain mountains where certain streams run and fishing for certain little red and black fish, the largest of which are a palm and a half long.[3] Therefore the Shah does not have falcons, because he does not take pleasure from them. His brother Bahrām is a magnificent man who takes much enjoyment and is always making festival in his house. He drinks a very great deal of aqua vitae and spirits of spices, as well as of cinnamon and spices. He has many handsome and finely dressed pageboys, among whom is one, called ʻAlī Jān, who has so many jewels in the turban-cloth round his cap that it is impossible to value them. The other brother too, Sām Mīrzā, only enjoys himself with his falcons; for the King does not give power to the said Sām Mīrzā; he only has the title, that they call him Emperor of Constantinople; and he has no beard. He is a young man of twenty eight years, stout and short. He has another brother, whose name is Alqās Mīrzā, whom he made King of Shīrvān, which was recently taken. The King has a sister in his house who he does not want to be married, because, he says, he is keeping her to be the wife of the Mahdī. This Mahdī is a descendent of ʻAlī and Muḥammad; and he says he keeps her on the

1 *Papasso*, from the Greek, is used here for priest.

2 Ṭahmāsp did hunt on occasion, as when entertaining the refugee Mughal prince Humāyūn. His fishing expeditions are occasionally mentioned in the Persian sources but are most fully described by Membré, below.

3 The fish were probably brown trout which occur in many rivers in Persia.

grounds that he is the court and the true place of Muḥammad. Thus, too, he has a white horse, which he keeps for the said Mahdī, which had a cloth of crimson velvet, and silver shoes; sometimes pure gold ones. No one rides this horse and they always put it in front of all his horses.

His stable-master is called *Mīrākhur*; he wears on his head a velvet cap without a cloth. And in the said court, a little distance behind his tents, he places all his horses in rows. There the servants who look after them are found; they are well-groomed and all with horse-cloths. They give them food in a nose-bag; and when they have eaten their barley, they take the said nose-bags off their heads and put bridles on them; and they tie the end of the bridle upon a tie which the saddle-cloth keeps tight; and they all stand with heads extended. The horses he had with him at that time were 89 in all, so far as I was able to count them.

The said Shah did not have a wife then; but he had two sons: one was in Khurasan, the other in Shiraz or Yazd. He married one of his sisters to a King who is near Shīrvān to the north, where Circassia is, close to Lawand Beg, the Georgian King, that is, in the city of Zagem. If I remember correctly the said Lordling is called the Beg of Shakkī. Another sister he has married to ʻAbdallāh Khān, who is at the confines of Baghdad. Another, as I heard, or a cousin, he gave as wife to the said Shāh qulī Khalīfa.

All the Sophians, that is men of the Sophy, wear the red cap, with twelve sections, by day, and by night the *Sulṭān-Ḥaidarī*, which *Sulṭān-Ḥaidarī* was worn by his grandfather. Then Shāh Ismāʻīl altered the fashion and made another form of cap, that is, of the form which appears below:

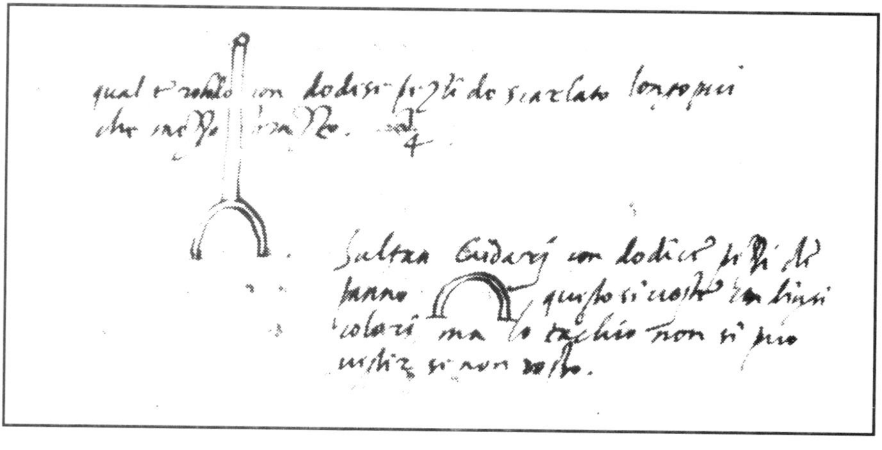

Figure. *Sketches of the* tāj *and the* Sulṭān-Ḥaidarī *(reduced) with the captions*: 1) This [the *tāj*] is a roll of scarlet, more than half an ell long, with twelve sections. 2) *Sulṭān-Ḥaidarī* with twelve sections of cloth. This is worn in diverse colours but the *tāj* can only be worn in red.

Those who are close to the King, those most loved by him, with whom he often talks and takes his pleasure, wear caps of black, red or green velvet. Their clothes are not narrow like those of the Ottomans, but wide, as if they are wearing *paigiami*. All of the King's *qūrchīs* wear swords with scabbards of massy gold - that is those *qūrchīs* who have done some deed of bravery - and the dagger, which they call *khanjar*, of massy gold with turquoises, and also all the Lords. And they wear a belt of massy gold with turquoises and rubies. They go well-dressed in velvet and brocade, which is made in the city of Yazd; and of these I have seen very many. They also wear on their heads, upon their turbans, a strip of gold with turquoise and ruby stones. And there are those of them who wear three or four gold strips; and they wear plumes, and at the foot of the said plumes there is massy gold with precious stones. And when the King makes any festival they all dress like this.

So, when the said Shāh Ṭahmāsp went to the said place in Marāgha, it could have been 12 or 16 leagues, always over meadows, for the horses, for at that time they were not giving the horses barley. So the Shah rode always on horseback as if he were on a field of battle, with sticks in his hand. The Shah is a good rider, from what I have seen. So, all that was in the month of September, if I am not mistaken, 1539.

After some days he had me summoned to his presence again, to where he was sitting in the pavilion of audience. In company with the above-named Sulṭāns, he began by asking me to be so good as to tell him the result of the league which the Most Illustrious Signory had formed, and of its strength, and of all things that were happening in the lands of the Franks, because he was eager to hear of them. I said to him what seemed good to me, in accordance with what I have written to the Most Illustrious Signory, and he answered me as appears in my letters directed to it; and he kept me in the audience until night had fallen. Then he gave me permission to leave, and I departed.

He himself went into certain mountains of the said Marāgha, on the summit of which pools of sweet water were to be found; and in the said pools many fish, as I have described them, were to be found; and the King went fishing. The chief of the fishermen is called Ḥusain Beg Chapnī. In the morning the King gets up and dresses himself in scarlet clothes, short garments, and with a *Sulṭān-Ḥaidarī* on his head. And he goes in company with 20 or 30 of his most beloved, and each one of them carries in his hand a thin cane, like those of fishermen. And with them they fish with hooks, and take their pleasure all day. So, afterwards each one of those who have caught fish submits them to the King's presence; and they make a heap of them; then he shares them among them and gives them what he likes; and the rest he sends to his kitchen. This fish has no bones and they fry it in fine oil, that is, butter, and eat it, for it is a very tasty fish. And he goes fishing throughout all those mountains.

Sometimes they block the course of the water and make it run on another side, and when the first channel is left empty, they catch the fish with their hands on the dry land. So, for the whole of October 1539 he went through all those places fishing.

Then he came down from the mountains to the plain, where he kept his horses and colts, and, with the *urdū*, passed through all those villages where he kept his horses. And, at each village, he stayed two or three days, outside in the plain. So he ordered that all the colts that were to be found in each place [should be presented to him], which was done; and he saw them one by one, and then, as they were brought, he allotted them to his vassals and *qūrchīs*, giving one to each of them to bring up and look after as a trust in the Shah's name. In this occupation he remained until 14 November.

News was coming from Tabriz that there was plague in that city and, on account of this pest he kept delaying the time [of return to Tabriz]. So, he ordered all the dogs to be killed. Then news came that the plague had ceased. On November 16 the Shah's brother, whose name is Bahrām, asked his brother the Shah for permission to go hunting, and he gave it to him. And he went, in company with the Sayyids of Uskū. So, after he had set out, the said Shah, talking to his vassals in the place of audience, said, 'I wish that the Lord God may do me this favour, that tomorrow it snows so much and is so cold that Bahrām will not be able to hunt.'

And so, while Bahrām had gone hunting, there were such snows and it was so cold that indeed he was very nearly frozen by such great cold and such terrible snows; and the said Bahrām returned without any game. The said snows and the cold lasted for three days.

So, the Shah gave permission for the court to go to Tabriz. And with such cold in the tent, with fur mantle and gloves I was unable to endure it. The servants could hardly fold the tents, stiff with snow and hard as boards, so much so that it seemed a marvel to me how they could load and arrange the cloth. Having seen this, it seems to me that the said men were born for this purpose. It was necessary that even I, although it was snowing, should go and travel with them. So I went in company with the household of Shāh 'Alī Sulṭān and Shāh qulī Khalīfa, with the camels. Thus, the little children were loaded on the camels: I do not know how they were not dried up like mummies with such cold. We crossed a river where I saw the servants strip and go in to help the loaded camels pass; and others went in with their clothes; then they exposed them to the wind and the clothes remained frozen. So, in this hardship, I did not observe that anyone died, save two or three men.

Chapter V

Tabriz. Persian Customs and Current Events.

At last we entered the city of Tabriz, in the month of December, if I am not mistaken, and the Shah stayed in his house for two days before coming forth to give audience. They were rebuilding the house of Shāh Ṭahmāsp which is in the said city. It is very beautiful, built within in a garden, and all around is a wall, one part of stone, another of thick earth; and it has two doors, one on the east, the other on the south-east. The part which is on the east has a square, which they call *maidān*, very neat and level and large; and in the middle of the said square there is a tall pole, which is of wood, with a gilded apple on the top. To the north stand two beautiful mosques, one next to the other; and, on the east, at the side of the said *maidān*, the said Shah is making anew another most beautiful mosque; so, on the side by the street runs a stream, which they call *chāy*. On the other side, to the south-east, is a wall, and within the wall a garden. So, on the other side, at the side of the said *maidān*, on the east, when one walks to go one's way by the King's palace, there stands the dwelling of his brother Bahrām Mīrzā; and in the other part, which is to the south-east, 19 paces beyond the gate, there is a bridge by which the street goes south-east; there, at the head of the street, stand the lodgings of the Sayyids of Uskū, all four together in one house. These are young men; the oldest is 37 or 38 years old.

Within the Shah's palace, the ways are divided off with bars of wood, because it is all gardens. So, porters with sticks stand at the doors. As for the first door, which is to the south-east near the bridge, as one enters the door, on the right hand is the station[1] of the Qūrchībāshī; then, on the left, is another door which goes to the treasury, which is where the goldsmiths are. So, on going straight on through the gate to pass the station of the Qūrchībāshī, going straight through, the garden is seen on one side and the other, dividing the paths, as I have said. Then, on the left hand, towards the chambers in which the Shah sleeps, there is the station of his brother, Bahrām Mīrzā, and, on the right, over against the station of the said Bahrām, is another station, that of Shāh qulī Khalīfa, who carries his seals on his breast on golden chains with many jewels. So, to turn a little to the east, there is then a great door straight ahead. Passing

1 Literally 'guard'; probably standing for Turkish (> Persian) *kishīk*.

on through the door, on the right hand is the station of his Minister, Qāḍī-yi Jahān; and, behind his station there is a high tower, all built of brickwork,[1] with a gateway with blue walls; and in the said tower are munitions, all in chests which they load two to a camel, all covered with leather; and in these chests are arrows, bows, swords and coats of mail, as I have seen. Then, as I have already said, passing by the station of the said Qāḍī-yi Jahān, and going further, there is another door, through which one passes to enter the court of the palace, where the Shah gives audience; and, on entering in the said little door, within there are certain vaults, where all his *qūrchīs*, that is cavalrymen, are seated on the ground with their swords; and passing on then, to the west, on the left, is the great fair palace, with four chambers, one behind the other, with their carpets and antechambers; and at all the doors stand porters, in accordance with the importance of the doors; for, in the said chambers they are seated all around the walls within, one next to the other; and so the room where the Shah is is very small and beautiful, all worked with azure and designs of foliage, as are all the chambers, with their vaults, and in the windows certain things which seemed to be panes of glass with figures in them. The second chamber is larger; along it sit his *Sulṭāns* of higher rank; in the third other *Sulṭāns* of lesser rank; in the fourth *qūrchīs* who stand in favour with the King, and are waiting to become *Sulṭāns*. So, the rooms in which the Shah sleeps are four by themselves, in the garden, towards the west. Near these chambers of his stands the bath. So, as one enters by the other door towards the east, where the *maidān* is, along either side are low walls; then, turning to the north, to the right, and going along a little to the right over the corner of the court, on the north-east there is the stable for the horses and below the stable, due east, his kitchen. So, from the kitchen by the way that goes direct to the palace towards the west, and within the garden near the other corner of the courtyard, to the north or north-east, there is a chamber where they make the spears and paint them; and a little below there is a little mosque where the Lords go and say their prayers. So, near the tower where the munitions are, as I have said, there is a square pool like a fishpond, made in the ground with stones, of 38 ells each side. It is full of sweet water, and in the water are four marble colonettes and on [each] one of the said colonettes there is a vault; and all around are screens of painted bars of wood. And the Shah goes upon it and takes pleasure fishing in the said water. There are plenty of fish there, and and a little boat, well provided with oars, its

1 The tower's proximity to the pool (below) indicates that the south-eastern, or *qibla, īvān* of the Mosque of 'Alī Shāh is meant. The vast brick structure, erected in the early fourteenth century, is still a landmark in Tabriz. It was being used as a mosque in the reign of Shāh Ismā'īl, and again in the seventeenth century, but its other possibilities were again appreciated in the nineteenth century, when it was used as fort, prison and military store by the Qājār governors of Ādharbāijān. It is popularly known as the Arg, or citadel.

poop with screens of bars of wood. So, when he wishes, he goes and takes his pleasure within in the garden.[1]

The said Shah entrusted me to the hands of the said Shāh qulī Khalīfa, the Muhrdār, and the whole time I frequented the houses of those Lords, that is Shāh qulī Khalīfa, the Qūrchībāshī, Qarā Khalīfa, Nāranjī Sulṭān, Taschiatan Masur, Qāḍī-yi Jahān, Shāhvirdī Dārūgha, Shāh ʻAlī Sulṭān and the Sayyids of Uskū. Thus, all of these used to take pleasure in talking with me and used to take me freely to their houses, and allow me to stay sometimes 15 or 20 days. And they took great pleasure in hearing about the affairs of Europe; for they knew nothing of those lands. Their wives are very beautiful and wear beautiful, big, round pearls at their necks. These ladies are very agreeable and keep all their husbands' money. When the husband wants something he has to ask his wife for the money. So the said Qizilbāsh love their wives a great deal. The ladies ride through the town like men and go with maids instead of grooms; and they go with the face covered with a white kerchief, so only the eyes are seen.

Through the months of December and January it was extremely cold, always snowing. Because of the cold, in the house they put a *tannūr*, that is a jar, but the bottom is wide and the mouth narrow; and they place it in the earth and leave uncovered the mouth, which comes to the level of the ground; and under the earth they make a kind of tunnel, with which is connected an opening in the bottom of the jar, so that a draught can enter and make the fire burn within; and in the said jar they put wood or charcoal and set it to burn. Then they sit all around the mouth, some putting their feet close to it and some their hands. And everyone has one like this in the chamber within in their houses, for otherwise they would not be able to survive through the great cold there is in those 3 or 4 months. And they often make flat loaves of bread and cook them inside the said jar; and in many houses these are their ovens.

In those days Shāh Ṭahmāsp banished his mother, who was called Tājlū Begum and had her confined in Shiraz, because he had been told, according to what I heard, that she wanted to poison him and make his brother Bahrām Mīrzā King. And the King learnt of the affair and took all she had from her, which was a great treasure. And he sent her away, accompanied by only three maids, and has given her 300 ducats a year to live on. He did not wish to kill her because his father had left it in his testament that he should never kill her, neither her nor any of his brothers.

---

1 A description of the Royal Boating Pool is given by the Venetian Merchant who was in Persia in the first decade of the reign of Ismāʻīl. From this and other sources it is evident that the pool was originally that of the courtyard of the Mosque of ʻAlī Shāh. (See the preceding note.)

On the first day of the month of February he holds a festival and it lasts three days.[1] For it, in the square where he is with his court, they place pavilions in rows, and the entrances of the pavilions are towards the east. For it there are most beautiful pavilions with columns gilded and with many figures. The pavilions are white outside but inside they are designed with much labour; and they lay fine carpets; and the King mounts, and in the said *maidān*, that is, piazza, he gallops his horse and plays at the wooden ball with the wooden bat, galloping on his horse. He places two pillars in the said *maidān* as marks, and they play in company, his brother with four men and the Shah with four others. So, each one has his pillar as a mark. So, the Shah aims to have his ball pass his pillar and his brother aims to have it pass his. And they gallop, hitting the said wooden ball, which is small, a little larger than an egg. And they ride and play in that way for two hours; and the people of the land and the soldiers, an infinite number, stand all around by the walls and in the street; and when they see the said Shah, they bow their heads to the earth and say, '*Shāh, Shāh*', as I have said.

So, during those three days, the Sophians come from the villages on foot, with their instruments and their *khalīfa*, 50 or 60 in a company. And they come into the said *maidān* and make a circle and begin to dance, one by one, and in twos, 3s and 4s. And the others play and sing praises to God and to Shāh Ṭahmāsp. And each one of the *khalīfas* carries a stick in his hand. And an infinite number of them come and many bring presents for the said Shah, some 10 wethers, some lambs, some horses, according to their means. For they say that the said Shah receives the tenth of what they earn each year, for being their prophet. And there are those of them who, when a daughter is born to them, say, 'She will be *nadhr* for the Shah,' that is a gift given for a vow. And when she is of suitable age, many bring her and show her to the said Shah, who keeps those who please him and lets the others go. And there are those of them who dedicate all they have to the Shah, and themselves go as hermits in his name. And in those days on which they hold those festivities, others sit and say, '*Lā ilāh illā Allāh*', that is make *dhikr*, praising God. And then the Shah gives food to many, that is, he sits at the pavilion where is his usual place, on a seat of gilded wood, covered with velvet; and they place on the ground in front of him dishes full of rice and mutton, which come to perhaps 3 or 4 thousand, so many that the said dishes take up 40 or 50 ells of the ground. The rice is part black, part blue, part red, part yellow and white; some of it they make sharp, or sweet, and of many kinds, all rice. The Lords his vassals are seated all around in the

---

1 The festival coincides reasonably well in date with the *'Īd-i fiṭr*, marking the end of the fast of Ramaḍān, which in 1540 fell on about 8 February. However, Membré does not mention any fasting and parts of the celebrations he describes are unorthodox. Like many Europeans of the period he did not realize that Islamic festivals are calculated by the lunar calendar, and so do not recur annually on the same solar date.

pavilions. It is already evening when they eat. And then the King goes into his house and all go their ways. But the Sophians who come to give praise stay the night and all night praise the said Shah, singing and playing. It lasts three days like this and then they go their way.

In that month a servant of Qarā Khalīfa led me to a place within the city of Tabriz, to a house which was on the square where the *naqqāra* sounds. And going through that street I found a house in which there was a clock, made by an old Persian with a white beard. The clock was constructed in a square casing of painted boards, enclosed with boards, and four ells high and two broad. The clock had these things: that is, on the top of the said cabinet it had a little bell, from which the hours were struck with a stick. This stood in the middle of the top of the cabinet. And at the front of the said cabinet were two men with horses and lances, as large as a hen, and two rams as big as a large rat, of the domestic kind. So, when it came to strike the hours, as many hours as the bell had struck, so many times did the men on the horses play at jousting with each other and the rams butt their heads against each other; and all this at one go. And it also had when the moon was going to be eclipsed. There was another thing too in the said clock: there was an orifice to which the ladies and the men went to find out their fortunes; and they used to put into the said orifice a copper farthing of their money, which they call *altun*. And that copper went down inside the said cabinet and a rumbling was at once heard, whereby a little door opened and a dragon came forth and voided from its mouth a little iron ball; and below that door another opened from which a cat-like creature came forth; and the said ball dropped into the mouth of the said cat. Then on the other side another door opened, and a serpent came forth and voided from its mouth a little sheet of inscribed paper; and they would read the paper and whatever the paper said, that would be their fortune. And I too tried my own fortune; and my sheet said that great riches would very soon come to me. So I am still waiting for them. I asked the said master who had made it if he had ever seen another like it, or if someone had taught him. He says that he had never seen one, and that no one had taught him, but that he had found such a thing only in books.[1]

The food of the Sophians, that is of the Lords, is always this: rices, *bughrā*, *qāvurma*, *qalya pilāv*, *qāvurma pilāv*, *qalya turshisi* [?], *sarī pilāv*, *kabāb-i jūja* and *shūrbā*. These are their pottages, all with rice where we would say macaroni. And they take the meat of wethers and cut it in little pieces and put a little water in the pot and leave it to cook and they cut onions fine and put them in with spices; that is both of them. For another, they cut the meat into very

1 The clock appears to be in the tradition of the clocks of the thirteenth-century Arab technician al-Jazarī and was probably water-powered. However, there is no precise model for it in al-Jazarī's work.

small pieces and put it to cook well, and then they put in rice and leave them to cook together; and they put in a few chick-peas and a certain bitter herb to make the rice blue; another one [is similar] but they do not put bitter things or colour in it. Another is similar, without rice but they put in little *zabībs*; another is rice with butter and saffron and white honey; so all their pottages are of rice. They also make roasts of the flesh of good, fat wethers and lambs, chickens, partridges and many other birds, but it is true that they are very dear. A lamb costs a ducat, a chicken a mozanigo. They do not eat hares. There is abundance of bread, barley, grapes and cherries; all other fruit are dear. Oranges are dear, for there are certainly none in Tabriz; nor do they come from Shīrvān. Pomegranates are dear; melons cheap in season and last until February, also grapes. The Sophians eat a fearful amount.

When a Sulṭān rides to go to court, there goes before him on foot a servant whom they call *shāṭir*; and he wears wide stockings to the knee and cloth breeches and a shirt of white cloth to the knee. And he has a little bell on the front of his belt; and another servant who carries his *fūṭa* on his shoulder together with a small carpet inside it, and in his right hand a silver flask with a long neck and a spout, full of water; and he goes before on foot; and another goes before carrying his bows and arrows, and him they call *ūkyāy-qūrchīsī*; and there are 20 or 30 other servants, some on horseback and some on foot; and all, when they arrive close to the Shah's gate, remain outside and do reverence to his gate, kissing the ground. And the Sulṭān dismounts at a distance and goes inside the court alone, together with the servant who carries the flask, with the *fūṭa* with the carpet in it on his shoulder. Because, when he wants to go into the palace where the King gives audience, he has to take off his shoes and the servant looks after them outside; and when he wishes to say his prayers in the mosque, he spreads his carpet on the ground and prays on it; and because they wash themselves with water they carry the said flask with them to wash with. So all do in this manner. When the Shah Ṭahmāsp eats in the palace, he gives food to all who happen to be in his company; and they put a dish of rice and meat, with much butter and fat, in front of each one. And then the servants serving at the King's table, who are called *farrāshs*, take what is left on the table before the said Lord and take it out to the door and call the servant of that Lord; and he runs and takes the dish, whether of silver or of porcelain, as it comes, and eats as much as he wishes and leaves the rest there with the said dish on the ground; and thus they all do. So then the servants of the King's table come and remove the dishes and basins, so no silver dish or basin is ever lost.

The King eats alone and his Sulṭāns watch, and then he shares out the dishes to everyone, because they bring all the food before him. As for the water he drinks, one of his *farrāshs* holds it in a jar of porcelain or silver, for I have seen two sorts of jar; and the King seals it with his seal, and when he wants to drink, unseals it, and, when the meal is removed, seals it up.[1] I have seen much confectionery at his court. A custom the said Shah has is that each day he gives a suit of clothes to his vassals, and some days three or four dresses. It is quite true that his dresses are not of very great value, because he does not take pleasure in wearing things of great price, but fine coloured bocasins, sometimes satins and sometimes brocades, of those made in Yazd, not others. He makes many gifts in money. When he makes a gift he gives 100, 200 and 300 *tūmāns*, each *tūmān* of which is worth 40 ducats. He pays his *qūrchīs* high wages, so that there are those of them that have 30 *tūmāns* a year; some have 10 and some 4 or five: these are the least there are. It is true that they have good horses and good arms for themselves and their horses; and they are edged weapons. They do not wear anything but cuirassines and coats of mail. During those days he gave Shāh ‘Alī Chapnī a gift of 100 *tūmāns* and gave him the city of Khuy and the fort of Van; and he made his son Dede Beg one of his *qūrchīs*.

During those days he sent his brother Bahrām Mīrzā with an army against a Kurdish Lord towards Mesopotamia; and the said Bahrām wished to take me with him, and we went. The Kurd fled and they fought little. A brother of his and a son were taken, and they were brought to the Shah's presence: and he had the head of the nephew cut off, and the beard [of the brother?]. And the said Bahrām Mīrzā depopulated all that country and took all the animals. And because some of the Shah's *qūrchīs* were not so ready to go on campaign and remained behind, Bahrām forthwith wrote to the King; and the said King immediately despatched Qarā Khalīfa and gave him orders that every one of those who had remained behind should ride backwards on a donkey, with bells every one, and come into the city and come riding thus to the presence of the Shah. So Qarā Khalīfa came with his orders, and the donkeys; and all those who had stayed behind rode the donkeys; among them was a carver at the Shah's table who rode a donkey. And another, called Kūpik-kirān [?], was pardoned because he was very dear to the King. So they came to the *maidān*, into the Shah's presence, and all the people ran to see them. And the Shah came forth from his apartments and began to question them and judge them; and they in return to clear themselves of the faults of which they were accused; and they stayed on the donkeys and finally left. And the Shah ordered each one to be given a suit of his clothes.

After that, after a few days, there came from Shīrvān two loads of heads stuffed with straw, three banners and four *rabābs*, that is tambourines, which the Shah's brother Alqās Mīrzā had sent, on having routed the Lords who had withdrawn to the forests and did not wish to give obedience. They were sent by the Shah to the middle of the square where justice is done and attached to a

1 A few years before there had been a plot to poison Ṭahmāsp's wine. He had, however, stopped drinking wine by this time.

gibbet, and the *naqqāra* sounded for three days and nights.

After this the Easter festival which they call Bairam was celebrated and many festivities were held, in the way I have already said: the pavilions placed in the *maidān* and polo played, as I have said above. And the next day, the King's Minister, Qāḍī-yi Jahān, gave a very great present to the Shah, which was, if I remember correctly, 9 fine horses with brocade horse-cloths and saddles of massy gold and with threads of gold in the middle of their hair; and 18 fine mules, and 36 very fine camels; and velvets, satins, many turban-cloths and cups of silver, bottles, gilded belts and I know not how much money in cash; so much so that I heard it said that the present was worth 1,000 tūmāns, which is 40,000 ducats.

The Shah's camels are very fine and strong, being called *techerech*, much better than those of Turkey; and similarly, the pavilions, arms, bows and arrows are very fine and good.

After that day had passed, the Shah went to eat in the house of his Minister, Qāḍī-yi Jahān, and he remained there for three days and then returned to his own house. And all the charges were paid by the said Minister, and I believe that more than 3,000 people ate in his house each day for certain.

On the first of April 1540 an envoy came to the court of the Shah in Tabriz, sent from Khurasan by a King of Khwarazm, whose name is Uzbek, that is from the wearers of the Green Hats; and the said King of Khwarazm is embattled with another King of the Green Hats, who is related to 'Ubaid Khān Uzbek, that is, of the Green Hats; and he took his brother and his nephew and cut off their heads and stuffed them with straw. So, with that envoy, the said King of Khwarazm sent the said heads to the Shah, saying he wished to be his vassal and put on his cap. So, the said Shah made festival: for three days and nights he had the *naqqāra* played from the square and he put the heads on the gibbet in the square. And after a few days the said Shah despatched an ambassador to the said King of Khwarazm, which is near Khurasan. And the ambassador of the Shah went in safety with many presents and pavilions, and many *tājs* and much rejoicing; and he was 2 months in returning. Then he came back with the brother of the said King of Khwarazm, who brought with him 40 or 50 of his men, who were all beardless; and the brother of the King was beardless. And I asked them why they did not sport beards; and many told me how that race cannot grow beards. And, with great honour, all the Lords of the land, and the Shah's brother went forth from the city[1] to meet the said brother of the King of Khwarazm, to accompany him; and they sounded the *naqqāras* of the land for three days and three nights.

---

1 According to Membré's dating of events the Shah would have left Tabriz by the time the King of Khwarazm's brother reached the court. The latter would have been welcomed to the Royal Camp rather than the city of Tabriz.

Then, in that month, two lesser Kurdish Lords, who were not in obedience to him, came and asked him for his cap, so as to be his vassals. He indeed gave it, and many presents, and they stayed a month and then departed.

All this time I was urging that I should be sent on my way, but I had no relief, for the Shah had ordered that an ambassador should be sent with me, one called Bairām Beg Chāvushlū, a man of much goodness, who was in the service of his brother Alqās Mīrzā in Shīrvān. And he ordered him to tell him to come for that purpose; so he delayed me from day to day. The ambassador urged more than me, for the said ambassador was, as it were, desperate because he could see no sign of his being sent off.

In that month a Sulṭān, who held the city of Qazvin[1] as governor, died. And the Shah set one of his *qūrchīs* in his place, a *qūrchī* who never in his life thought that the Shah would make him a Sulṭān. So, one day when the said *qūrchī* was in his own home he ordered him to be summoned; and he went, not thinking anything of it. And at once, a Sulṭān's clothes, as is the custom, were given to him; and he also gave him the whole household of the Sulṭān who had died, as it was, with goods, money, draperies, animals and everything; and he also gave him the governorship of the city of Qazvin, and his wife, and made him Lord of everything in the space of an hour. And in all the land that day they took this for a miracle. It was true that the said *qūrchī* had done many valiant deeds and had brought many heads to the said Shah, but he had never given him presents; the said man was always thus, not thinking he was in the Shah's favour. And that was in the month of April 1540.

---

1 Apparently the name of the city is given as Casilia and Casilian in this passage, but the story is also given by Ḥasan Rūmlū, whose grandfather, Amīr Sulṭān, was the Governor of Qazvin who had just died. Rūmlū, not necessarily impartial on the matter, describes the new Governor, Pīr Sulṭān Khalīfa, as of exceptional stupidity.

Chapter VI

Further observations on the Court, Life at Tabriz and Current Events.

I, as I have already said, all that time had very much converse and friendship with all at the court of the said Shah, especially with his brother Bahrām Mīrzā, who many times had me called at night when he was feasting, to enjoy himself talking with me and showing me their *ṣuḥbat.* And at his board he had instruments: tambours, psalteries and flutes, *dunbaks* and a small lyre; and a very handsome boy who sang very well to the instruments. So, he had in his company those men, that is, Nāranjī Sulṭān, Kachal Shāhvirdī Beg and Qarā khalīfa, and a Sayyid from Khurasan; and of young men there were 'Alī Jān and Shāh Khurram [?] and another boy from Shīrvān, all three sitting one next to the other. Three others, who were older, were on the other side; one of them was his *parvānachī*, who got married during those days; and the said Bahrām Mīrzā made a great feast in certain apartments, and put up many tents in a square where he held the feast.

And on the night when Bahrām Mīrzā summoned me to his repast, as I have said, those three boys were seated on one side, and the others, that is, his *parvānachī* and the other two, his *sufrachīs*, on the other side; the musicians on another side and he himself facing the said 'Alī Jān. They were all thus seated on fine carpets, where his lodgings are, behind his apartments to the north towards the garden. So all that night he made *ṣuḥbat*, they drinking much aqua vitae and spirit of cinnamon, wherefore he became drunk and stretched himself out to sleep. Then the musicians left, and we others, and there remained only the two young men, drunk, stretched out on the carpets on the ground. That was after midnight. Then we went to the house of Nāranjī Sulṭān to sleep, because his lodgings were in the street nearby. The next day he asked me if I had been drunk. I said not and he marvelled greatly. So he planned to summon me another time, to make me drunk, and I was never willing to go to him; and for that reason he was half disappointed with me.

As I was talking to the Sayyids [of Uskū], they said that I should tell them why the Venetians had a lion for their arms; for they marvelled much at that, saying that the lion belonged to the Shah, for 'Alī is an invisible lion. To men it appeared that he was a man, but he was a lion, sent by God to destroy the idolators. So, in their histories, the arms of 'Alī are represented as a lion. That

was why they wished to know. Wherefore I replied that from this they could see by trial whether the Signory was a friend of the Shah or no; for they have such love for ‘Alī that they carry his arms and adore him, and are more devoted to him than others. He said to me that I must tell him how that had come to pass. I said to them,
'At the time when ‘Alī was alive, although in these parts he was in the form of a man, in the parts where Venice is he used to go in the form of a lion and appeared so visibly; and he spoke of the word of God in the ears of holy men, of God's miracles and heavenly things. So they wrote it all down, which has made a book, which they now call Gospel, and in Turkish *Injīl.*'
And he said to me that they admitted that the said Gospel was true, and they too believed in the said *Injīl*. And with that they were left well-informed by me; and they said that it would be right that they should call me *muvālī*, that is one beloved of ‘Alī; and that it would be a greater crime to kill a Venetian than a thousand Ottomans

Their food is like that of the Turks, but it is certainly true that they are of greater liberality and sincerity, and have people to eat in their houses more than the Ottoman people.

When one of them dies they go to bury him with the companies,[1] that is, with black banners, without figures, with gold designs of foliage, and with tassels all round the said cloth. And on a spear they put certain branches, like a tree, and place [on them] many red oranges, and go with *dunbaks*; and they also make a catafalque of planks, small enough for four men to be able to carry it; and on top of the said box they place a little boy who can read the Koran, and he goes along chanting it. And he goes accompanied by many men; and if he is a soldier of the King, they bring in their company his horse, caparisoned with all his arms. Then they place them in their mosque. And if he was a man who was in the Shah's favour, he orders him to be buried in the city of Ardabil.[2] And I know this because at that time a brother of Tachiatan Massur had died and, because he was the Shah's *qūrchī*, he ordered him to be buried in the said Ardabil, which would be three days from Tabriz, to the east. So, I saw this, as I have already said; and on that day all the Lords went to the house of the said Mansur, the brother of the dead man, to comfort him and I myself went too.

1 *Scolle.* The editors take the word to be from Persian *shāl*, shawl, and to refer to the banners but *shāl* does not seem to used in this sense. Here it is assumed to be the Venetian form of Italian *scuole*, commonly used for the religious fraternities of Venice. Cf. p. 43 below, where the reading is *scole*.

2 Ardabil was the home of Ṣafī al-Dīn, the Sufi Shaikh with whom the Safavid family first came to prominence. His shrine there was held in reverence by the Safavid Shahs and their followers. Its graveyard still contains a number of fine carved 16th-century gravestones, which support Membré's assertion.

Thus, his dwelling is towards the south-east and east, that is, if one wishes to go to his house from the house of Qarā Khalīfa, from the square of the *maidān* where the *naqqāra* sounds, it is by the street which goes directly east, which will be near a Sayyid. For the Sayyid sits on the street, writing petitions and producing letters for people; and there is a little doorway on the left; so one passes that door and enters that strait street: the dwelling of the dead man was there. So I went too, in Qarā Khalīfa's company, to console him and because he had been my friend.

In those days there came a great Lord of Gilan, who was Lord Soprasi, who had been driven from his lands by another Lord of the said province of Gilan; and he came to Tabriz to present himself to the Shah. So, the Shah sent all his Lords forth from the city to escort him and ordered him to be given his cap, and clothes and gifts: so he made great festival and promised to give him the army to go and seize his own lands, and also to destroy his enemy. So, when he entered the city he had those *tabarrā'īs*, who cried out, praising the Shah and cursing the Ottomans.

The Shah wears his cap with the turban-cloth, that is, the cap is covered to its top by the cloth, which is twisted round it from the bottom and ties up the whole of it. So, all those who receive a cloth as a favour wear it so for three or four days and then tie it another way. They call this manner of tying it *Shāh-destūri*; the Sayyids of Uskū wear the *tāj* as the Shah does, also Qāḍī-yi Jahān, the Shah's brothers and the *qūrchīs*, but not others. And none can wear a velvet *tāj* unless the Shah gives it, nor have a belt or flask of gold, nor plumes on the head, nor a sword with a gold scabbard. And the Shah is always giving all those things to everyone, and granting them to those who deserve favour. At that time I saw a Turk of Anatolia come to the Shah's court asking for one of the Shah's turban-cloths, which he is accustomed to give for a high price; and for that cloth they give him a horse as a gift. And this happens secretly. I know it because there came one from Anatolia, that is from Adana, and he came to the Lord in whose house I was staying, that is Shāh qulī Khalīfa, and brought a bag of fine dried figs as a present for him, and begged him to speak to the Shah, so that he should give one of his kerchiefs. And he had, to give as a present to the said Shah, a horse. So the said Shāh qulī Khalīfa, with great difficulty, was able to get the said cloth; he it was who presented the horse. And when the said Turk saw the cloth, he raised his hands to heaven and praised God, and bowed his head to the ground and said, '*Shāh, Shāh* ', and was overjoyed. So he took the said cloth and went his way. I asked him what the cloth was good for, and he told me that it was a *tabarruk*, that is, an object of beneficial effect; and, having a sick father at home, he had seen the said Shah in a dream; and for that reason he wished for the cloth, for his father's contentment, for he would be well. Every year many such people come, but they go in secret, so none can know, except he be a man of that court.

I saw another man come from Khurasan, asking with much insistence for one of the shoes which the Shah wears; wherefore he came to the house of the said Shāh qulī Khalīfa. So he stayed a month to be able to get the said shoe; and in my presence he put it in cotton, kissing it a hundred times, and touched it to his eyes, and was overjoyed. Then His Lordship [Shāh qulī Khalīfa] told me that with that shoe of the Shah he gained his living, showing it to the Turcomans, who out of devotion gave him wherewith to live and that if he found some of them sick they asked for it and gave him money. So, the said man from Khurasan took the shoe and went his way. The eldest son of Qarā Khalīfa fell ill and in my presence he sent to the Shah's court to ask for some of the water with which the Shah washes his hands. After his hands are washed the water which remains, which we others throw away, he keeps. So they gave him a little in a silver flask and he drank it to cure himself; for they say that it is holy water, so they only give the said water to those who are great men.

When the Sophians wish to swear they say '*Shāh bāshısı*', that is, 'By the head of the Shah', and when one wishes to return thanks to another, they say '*Shāh murādın versi*', that is, 'May the Shah give him his desire.' And when they are going to ride they say '*Shāh*', and when they want to dismount they say '*In, Shāh.*' So, in those parts, nothing is heard but '*Shāh*'. They say that the said Ṭahmāsp is the son of ʻAlī, although ʻAlī has been dead for 900 years.[1] All the Lords that want to render thanks to the Shah, whether in his presence or his absence, bow their heads to the ground and say '*Shāh, Murtaḍā ʻAlī.*'

I have often been at their weddings, during which, the first thing that they do when they gather, they all sit in rows in a room, from one end to the other, seated on fine carpets, and they begin to praise God and then Shāh Ṭahmāsp. The *khalīfa* begins first; so all are singing '*Lā ilāh illā Allāh*,' and they go on with that phrase alone for a whole hour; then they begin to sing certain songs in praise of the Shah, composed by Shāh Ismāʻīl and the said Ṭahmāsp, called κατaι, that is *khaṭā'ī*; and after that is done, there sits one with a tambour, and he begins to call very loudly the names of all those who are there, one by one; and then each one whose name he calls says '*Shāh bāsh*,' that is 'The Shah is head',[2] and all of them give to the one who calls the name, money, depending on how much courtesy each one wishes to show. And after that is done, the *khalīfa* has a substantial wooden stick, and begins from the first to the last; one by one they all come for love of the Shah to the middle of the room and stretch themselves out on the ground; and the said *khalīfa* with the stick gives them a most mighty blow on the behind; and then the *khalīfa* kisses the head and feet of the one he has given the blow; then he himself gets up and kisses the stick; and thus they all do, one by one; so, as I was sitting there, it then came to be my

1 ʻAlī died on 25 January AD 661.

2 See Glossary, *Shāh bāsh*.

turn, and the villain, who had a pair of cloth breeches, gave me a blow which still hurts. And they do that because the Shah has ordered it so, because none of his *qūrchīs* can marry without the permission of the Shah, who it is that makes the rules for the weddings; it is said that that blow signifies the first letter of their abc, which they call *alif, bā', tā', thā'*, that is, like this: ا، ب، ت، ث. So, when that is done they begin to sound the tambour and other instruments and sing songs in disparagement of the Ottomans, and how they came to Tabriz and lost all their artillery,[1] with many other stories; and how the Shah is to go into the lands of the Ottomans, and how he will make war and many other lovely things. Then they all dance, in twos, threes and fours, men in one room and women in another, for the men do not go with the women. And then they eat and go their way; and thus they make their weddings.

In the month of May they perform the passion of a son of 'Alī, wherefore they call him Imām Ḥusain, who fought with a certain race which they call Yazīd, and had his head cut off; for that martyrdom they perform the passion for ten days, and for it they all wear black, black turban-cloths and black clothes. For those ten days the Shah does not come forth from his house. From evening to one hour of the night the companies[2] go round through the city and through the mosques chanting in Persian the passion of the said Imam Husain. This they call *'Āshūrā'*, that is ακιουρ. And that began on I May, up to the tenth.[3] I saw young men make their bodies black and go naked on the earth. I saw another thing on the square which they call after the Begum,[4] someone make a hole underground like a well, and put himself in it naked and leave only his head out, with all the rest in the hole, packed in with earth up to the throat; and that was to perform that passion. This I saw with my own eyes. In the evening all the ladies betake themselves to their mosques and a preacher preaches the passion of the said son of 'Alī, and the ladies weep bitterly.

Then, when the said *'Āshūrā'* was over, Shāh Ṭahmāsp ordered his *kārkhāna*, that is, his pack camels loaded with his court furniture, and went east towards Ūjān, on the road that goes to Sultaniyya, where there was much green herbage. So the Shah intended to go forth. And after all the Lords saw that the court was going forth, they too sent their camels with their chests; so, for three days and nights the said pack camels and mules kept passing, an infinity of them. On 20 May 1540 the Shah rode towards Ūjān, where he situated his court. After two

---

1 In the autumn of 1534 the Ottoman army had occupied Tabriz and was advancing further eastwards when an early snowstorm forced Sulaimān to retreat towards Baghdad, abandoning part of his artillery.

2 *Scole*. See p. 40 n. 1 above.

3 *'Āshūrā'*, 10 Muḥarram, 947 fell on 19 May 1540.

4 Like the bazaar of the Begum mentioned below (p. 51) the square may have been called after the wife of Jahānshāh Qarāquyūnlū.

days two lesser Kurdish Lords came and asked the said Shah for his *tāj*, for they wished to become his vassals; and they gave them many presents, and he kept festival for three days, sounding the *naqqāra*.

Chapter VII

The failure of the Mission. The journey to Hormuz.

After that had happened, news came from Constantinople by his spies that the Ambassador of the Most Illustrious Signory of Venice was at the court of the Turk, asking for peace; so I found myself to be in disgrace with the whole court, because at that very time the said King had prepared everything to despatch me with the appointed ambassador, as I have said before, and to send him with me.

And after that had passed, the King's court kept moving to meet the said Ghāzī Khān[1] with an army of, if I remember well, about 2,500 horsemen. And he depopulated that province of Baghdad, carrying away with him the households with the women, animals and everything; and by what was said there were women 4,000 in number. So, having seen that, the said Shah made great festivities and had the *naqqāra* sounded for 3 days. So, the said Ghāzī Khān came in company with his army to kiss the foot of the said Shah, together with the above-mentioned army of his. So, they stood opposite the court of the said Shah at a distance, all on horseback with their arms and cried out, '*Allāh, Allāh*', which is to say, 'God, God'; and crying out thus they came little by little down so that the said Shah would order him to be summoned. So, after an hour had passed, he ordered him to be summoned; and he came alone with a present to give to the said Shah: there were camels, 45 in number, fine horses 25,[2] mules 36, lances of Babylonia about 200, slaves 9 in number and gold coins in a little bag, the quantity of which I do not remember. So, he kissed the King's foot and the King had him given a suit of vestments of great price; and then he had the men of the said Ghāzī Khān summoned one by one, and they kissed the feet of the said Shāh Ṭahmāsp. So the said Shah spent three days banqueting with many festivities. And so the said Ghāzī Khān ordered me to be summoned and spoke with me, and was much pleased; and he promised to see that the King should send me off. And so I was sent off in the course of those days.

1 Ghāzī Khān has not been mentioned previously in the *Relazione*, but his name does occur in Membré's despatches. Persian accounts place his arrival at Sūrlūq, now generally known as Takht-i Sulaimān.

2 It was an originally Turkish practice, considered lucky, to give gifts in multiples of nine, so there should be 27 horses. Cf. the figures for Qaḍī Jahān's present for the Shah on p. 36.

And that was in the month of August 1540.

After that month I set off from the court of the said Shah, as I have reported in full by my letters by special courier. So I left the said Shah most greatly occupied because he wanted to send an army against a Kurd, called Ḥājjī Shaikh, that is, κατι κιεκυ, because they said he was doing great damage on his frontiers by being strong. So he ordered those Lords to be sent off, that is, 'Abdallāh Khān, Shāh Sulṭān [?], Muḥammad Sulṭān, Ghāzī Khān and his brother Bahrām Mīrzā. The Lord in whose house I stayed, Shāh qulī Khalīfa, Gūkcha Sulṭān, those Lords were listed to go with his army; and the day that I set out they too were about to leave; so, what was the outcome, I do not know.

Then I in company with two Moors made my way to the city of Qazvin, passing a city which was called Nuacar,[1] with many gardens; and I also passed beside Sultaniyya. So, at the end of about nine days I entered the city of Qazvin; which city is near certain mountains of Gilan, a great city with many gardens and much abundance of provisions; however, the water is bad, and the air, for all the citizens have fever in summer. So I stayed one day. Then on the following day we went our way, always travelling alone, and again a level road; and there were many melons by the road. So, from the said place Qazvin we went to another city which they call Qum, a large place, but there are many ruined shops and houses there; and we were 4 1/2 days on the road, and stayed in the said city for two hours until the heat passed. Then, in the cool we travelled on in the way I have said: we travelled always a level road, without mountains, and every 3, 4, 5 or 6 leagues there were villages. So, we always travelled by night; by day we slept in the open country. We used to buy victuals from the villages, barley, bread and other things to eat, and put them in our panniers; and so long as it lasted we did not enter a village, but always went outside.

And then we entered a city called Kashan, that is κακιαν. Which city is surrounded by a wall of earth and is a great and mercantile city, but the waters are a little dismal. There are many fruits there and most of all melons. Much silk comes to the said city from Gilan, Varāmīn, Shīrvān and Mazandaran, for at the said city they load the caravans and go to Hormuz. So I lodged in a caravanserai at the edge of the said city, toward the east, where the road to Isfahan goes. So I stayed in the said caravanserai for 3 or 4 days, and on the road from the city of Qum to Kashan I was 5 days, and from the city of Kashan to Isfahan 4 days. On the said road from Kashan to Isfahan we suffered for water, because in one place there were 8 leagues that we could not have water because the land was salt and desert; and twice there were 8 and 9 leagues

---

1 Zanjān? Or possibly Abhar, though it is after Sultaniyya.

without there being villages. As I have said, we always travelled over level country.

Then we entered the said city of Isfahan. Which city was surrounded by a wall of earth; and near the outer gate passed a great conduit of sweet water. Wherefore the said city is very beautiful and there are many waters and gardens, and many fruits, the finest water and abundance of provisions. In that city I was sick of the fever for about 25 days, during which the said two Moors took care of me well, as if I had been a brother. And during that time, two lesser Lords of the court of the Sophy entered that city with their slaves and servitors; and the said two Moors of mine saw them in the square and went to them and told them of what had happened. They at once came to me and took me away to their dwellings and looked after me with physics and with much care for about 10 days. Then they provided for my expenses, for me and the Moors, and set me on my way. So we left the said city, if I am not mistaken, in the month of October 1540. And as I have already said, outside the city are many waters and gardens.

And we travelled two days over plains, and then we entered certain deserts, which were 6 leagues long; and in that desert there were so many flies that they came near to killing our horses, in such a way that the blood ran from their bellies as with a phlebotomy. And after we had passed the said deserts we came into certain mountains, not very large, full of small trees; and we travelled through the said mountains for half a day. Then we entered hills as far as Shiraz, so that from Isfahan to Shiraz we were 6 days on the road. The said city of Shiraz is encircled by a wall of earth; which city has many gardens; it is large but much ruined. There is abundance there and freedom for strangers to drink wine, and many fair courtesans, while in no other city is there this freedom. Then we stayed in that city about four days, or five; then I departed with my said Moors and we went to the city of Lar. On the way there we passed many date palms, innumerable. On the way we were 4 1/2 days on the road, always travelling over plains and hills.

Then we entered the city of Lar, in the month of November 1540. Wherefore the said city is half encircled with a wall of stone, that is the city within together with the fortress is encircled with a wall; which city is half on high and the other half below; and outside the city are other houses without a surrounding wall. So we lodged in one of the caravanserais that were without, which caravanserai was opposite the square without. And in the said city are many water citadels,[1] and all drink from the said citadels and carry water in skins on donkeys. And in the said city are inns of whores. Their King there is King Soprassi, but he is a vassal of the Sophy; and they speak Turkish and Persian. The said King wears the Sophy's cap. The goldsmiths of the said city

1 So, consistently, for cisterns.

are Gentiles[1] from India and they wear on their heads a white cloth, narrow and long, with which they bind their heads; and on the forehead they carry a red mark, as of a red dye, to be known as Gentiles among the Moors.[2] So they all live together in one street.

And in the said city we sold our horses and went by hire with the caravan to Hormuz, being 4 1/2 days on the road. On the road were many water citadels, for otherwise water was not to be found. So every two leagues there was a citadel and a caravanserai without doors, for the caravans to go and lodge within. And there were many of those caravanserais as beautiful as inns, and so also citadels of water up to near the city of Hormuz, which is by the Indian Sea or Sea of Hormuz. So the said Moors of Lar make those citadels and those inns on the road for their souls. For, when they die, those who have money leave orders to build them, some leaving orders to build an inn, some leaving orders to build a citadel. So, in the said city of Lar, as I have said, at night they leave the shops closed with certain canes or certain fine sticks bound with string as doors; and within they are full of goods. So they are not afraid of thieves, because the said King of Lar does great justice. Then we set off from that city and we travelled about four days, always over plains, and we passed by a certain place like a gorge, a mountain on one side and the other, and level below, and the road was down in the said plain.

So we came to the sea, in that place by the sea which is called Bandar of Hormuz; which Bandar had houses of straw and of date wood, about 70 or 80 in number. So the merchants lodge in certain houses called *nuzl*, which are, as it were, hostels. And the women of the said Bandar are like blacks; and they put a silver ring in their noses, and so also in the ears. The shops of the said place all belong to half-black Gentiles, with a white cloth on their heads. So then we stayed one day and the next day, half an hour before sunrise, we boarded a boat, and at two hours of the day arrived at Hormuz. And that was the 12, 13 or 14 of November, if I am not mistaken, on Sunday, if I remember well; and then, as soon as I was in the land of Hormuz, in the city, I went to listen to what the Portuguese were saying, and I placed myself next to some Portuguese merchants to hear what they were saying; and, not being able to understand their tongue, I was left desperate: I decided to go towards the fortress, for it stood towards the sea, in the part towards Persia, so as to be able to find someone who could speak Italian. I found a Jew who was the interpreter of the Captain the fortress; and not realizing that he was a Jew, for he wore a headdress like the Moors, I decided to ask him if he knew any Italian merchant who traded in that land, for I wished to talk with them. He replied asking what I wanted to talk to merchants about and what business I had with them. I told

1 Hindus, as opposed to Muslim 'Moors'.

2 Hindu 'caste-marks'.

him that I wanted to deal with them in certain jewels in which I was trading. So he took me to a Messer Francesco, a German, who could speak Italian well.

And then the said Jew went along to the house of the Captain, who was called Messer Martin Alfonso de Melo, a Portuguese, and told him of what had happened. Then he said to him that it seemed to him that I was a spy of the Turk. At that time I was speaking with the said Messer Francesco Alemano,[1] and I told him that he must go to the Magnificent Captain and say that I was Ambassador of the Most Illustrious Signory of Venice and of His Magnificence the Emperor, wherefore I was coming from the Shāh Ṭahmāsp Sophy; that I begged him with great insistence to allow me to be sent on the ship, which at that time they were about to send for the Kingdom of Portugal, and that I beseeched him to send me at once, which was for the benefit of Christendom. Therefore the said Messer Francesco Alemano at once went into the fortress where the Captain himself lived and told him what had happened. So, as I have said already, the Jew had told him that I was a spy of the Turk. The said Messer Captain replied to him that I must go to him for him to see me. So the said Messer Francesco came back to me and told me what the said Captain had ordered. So I at once, that very day towards evening, went to the house of the said Captain in company with the said Messer Francesco Alemano. So the said Captain saw me willingly and asked me whence I came. I told him how I was coming from the court of the Sophy, and I begged him to give me help to go by the ship of the King of Portugal. The said Captain wondered to see me in such bad state, being ambassador on such a great enterprise, although he had the news before from the caravans which came to Hormuz from Tabriz, which said that there was at the court of the Sophy a young Venetian as ambassador. So it seemed strange to the said Captain and he asked me. I told him how in the desert of Shiraz the robbers had stripped me and taken everything there was, and killed one of my companions whom the Sophy had given me to accompany me; and that I, wishing to go quickly to my own country, had not wanted to go back, for it was already a great distance. So the said Captain believed me. Then he asked me about the two Moors I was bringing in my company. I said to him, 'One is my servant, who was an Arab of Tunis; the other the Sophy has given me to take with me to the Most Illustrious Signory, and, as I have said, he gave me another companion who was killed by the robbers.'

So the said Captain was left thus: he half believed and half disbelieved.[2] And that night I went away. In the morning he ordered my food for me well and also sent a tailor to measure me for clothes to be cut for me. And that day

---

1 Alemano meaning German.

2 It may not be obvious at first reading that Membré, to win the Governor's sympathy, has improved his story to explain why he is travelling so modestly, without fully revealing the reasons.

passed well. That night he had me summoned by 20 or 21 soldiers, during which he told me that I must show justification and testimony that I was ambassador. Otherwise he would take judicial proceedings against me. For they had become doubtful that I might not be a spy of the Lord Turk. So I replied to him with many arguments and showed him letters which I had with me for the said Lords, and said how there were two ambassadors of the Sophy in the said place Hormuz, great men with many presents, as the said Captain knew well, who were about to go to India on an embassy to an Emperor called Humāyūn Pādishāh. Thus one of them they called Khwāndamīr Āqā, and the other Ḥusain Āqā; and by the letters, and the account of the said ambassadors the truth could be known. So the said Captain, Messer Martin Alfonso de Melo, kept the letters in his hands and ordered me into arrest with the guards all night; and the Moors he placed one separate from the other. So the said Captain took counsel with his counsellors that night, and in the morning he had the said ambassadors of the Sophy summoned and asked them if they knew the ambassador who was at the court of the Shah. They answered yes and he showed them the letters and they attested to him that they were from their Sophy.

So that morning he ordered me new garments in the Portuguese fashion, and had me dress in them; then he had me summoned, in company with three or four young men of (if I am not mistaken) my age, to the chamber in which he was sitting with his counsellors and the said ambassadors of the Sophy. So, at my entering by the door of the chamber, the said ambassadors recognized me, rose to their feet and embraced and kissed me and said, 'This is he whom our Lord, and all his court held most dear, because he has done deeds of valour.' Thus they vouched for me; and, notwithstanding that, they gave oaths on their Koran, swearing that it was the truth that I had carried letters with the golden seal to the Sophy, and all accepted me as ambassador and held me dear. So, instantly the said Captain embraced me and kissed me and begged my pardon, saying it was his custom to do thus, because he was on the frontier of Persia. So that hour passed and then he provided me with a meal and in the evening, at the setting of the sun, he ordered me to be given 90 ducats of gold, clothes of crimson satin and brown damask, shirts and victuals to eat on the ship, a pallet and sugar conserves. And he accompanied me to the ship with two great wax tapers and about 30 or 20 soldiers; and they put me in the boat. To each one of the Moors he gave clothes and 20 ducats and he sent them with me; and the Captain of the said ship was called Farnando Lintu. We set off on the 14th or 15th of the month of November, if I am not mistaken, in 1540. So we sailed along, always with bad weather, and in the ship they kept me good company.

Chapter VIII

Digression on the City of Tabriz. To India. Description of Hormuz. India, and the Voyage to Portugal.

But to go back in my account, as regards the city of Tabriz, its money; this is certain silver aspers which weigh a *sazo* and a half; and six of those aspers, which they call *shāhī*, make a gold ducat. And they make another kind of money like Turkish aspers, which they call *ghāzībegīs*, money of copper, as large as a bagatin, and also one a little larger which they call *pūl*. So, two of these make an *altun* and 50 *altun* make a *shāhī* of silver; also gold ducats like *Sulṭānis*; so, all their coins are confirmed by legends of theirs on them.

At the entrance to the city of Tabriz from Anatolia it is all gardens and mosques with blue vaults, and on the way out on the road to Khurasan to the east is the square where the *naqqāra* plays. In the said square there is a gibbet, always full of heads stuffed with straw, and the *ṣarrāfs*, that is those who change money, sit there with their counters. In the said square there is also a bath on the east, another on the south east, a caravanserai on the north, one on the east and two on the west. They are like inns. So, on passing the square to go directly east through the bazaar called the Begum's, and going straight to the end of the said bazaar, there is a mosque with two minarets, which are like tall bell-towers.[1] This mosque is so well built that neither in the land of the Turk, nor in all the lands I have seen, have I found another such building. Outside is all designs of foliage like porcelains, and with beautiful coloured marbles. So, I have seen, in the top of one of its domes there was a copper apple, in which there were three arrows which had been shot by the *sipāhīs* of the Grand Turk, when he entered Tabriz. So, behind that mosque there is a very large garden, full of almond trees; and in that garden there is a most beautiful stream, and one healthy to drink; opposite the said mosque is the dwelling of an Arab Sayyid of Baghdad, and next to his dwelling is a bath-house. Then that straight road, passing over a small bridge, goes out of the city on the way to Khurasan and

1 From its decoration and position on the east of Tabriz the building is evidently the Blue Mosque, built by Jahānshāh Qarāquyūnlū (d. 1467) and his wife Khātūn Jān Khātūn, known as the Begum, meaning the Lady. The bazaar of the Begum, and the square of the Begum mentioned earlier (p. 43) were probably parts of the same complex and called after her.

Iraq. Facing the said city to the north are red mountains and, on the summit of a blue hill a little fort has been built, inside a great mosque; the said mountains are without trees, and are black, red and, below, blue.

In the said city firewood is very dear and they do not use it, but the dung from the stables of the horses and other animals. Charcoals are very dear; thus I have seen a ducat asked for a camel-load of firewood. And that is because the mountains of the said places are all bare; it is necessary to go two days' distance to bring wood. The Sophians make their prayers like the Moors but the former curse those whom the Turks bless in their prayers. The Sophians make their prayers wherever they happen to be and the Moors, if they are in a city that has a mosque, make their prayers there, but the Sophians do not worry about that. All the Sophians go about with swords, as in Spain.

The Sophians paint figures, such as the figure of 'Alī, riding on a horse, with a sword; and when they see the said figure of 'Alī, they take hold of their ear and bow their head, which is a kind of reverence. In their squares there are many Persian mountebanks sitting on carpets on the ground; and they have certain long cards with figures; and the said mountebanks hold a little stick and point to one figure after another, and preach and tell stories over each figure. So everybody gives them some money. There are also others with books in their hands, reading of the battles of 'Alī and the combats of the Princes of old, and of Shāh Ismā'īl; and all give money to hear. Others, called *tabarrā'īs*, are to curse the Ottomans and sing songs of how the Shah is to go to Constantinople and place his brother Sām Mīrzā there as King, and many other ceremonies; and all give them money. Thus I have seen one of those *tabarrā'īs* take one of the Ottoman merchants, take him by the beard and say, 'Curse the Ottomans'; and he pulled it so hard that he cursed them a hundred times. So the Ottomans in Tabriz live with the Sophians as cats live in the company of dogs. The streets of the city are very narrow and most of the houses are partly underground; and while indeed they do not appear large they are beautiful, painted inside and neat, with their gardens.

And to return to my story, after setting out in the said ship of Hormuz, I was at sea for 35 or 40 days before coming to the coast of India. So, we touched at a land they called Muscat, where there is a town of Moors[1] beside the sea, at which we watered; for the ship was loaded with horses, 90 in number, so it needed water;[2] in the said Muscat there is a river and near the river are sugar canes.[3] In the said Muscat they catch so many fish that even the animals eat

1 Muscat was in the possession of the Portuguese.

2 As Membré says below, the island of Hormuz has no water supply of its own.

3 There is no river at Muscat town. Ships watered from a tank fed by a modest conduit from inland springs. Even if Membré stopped elsewhere in the teritory of Muscat, for instance at nearby Mutrah, the river, and the sugar cane, are difficult to explain.

them. I have even seen houses and walls built of dried fish.

So we departed from the said place in bad weather, and, as I have already said, we were 35 or 40 days before touching land, at which time we had no more water and if we had been two more days without touching land all the horses would have died of thirst. So, the Lord God provided that we touch land at a city near Diu, which they called Patan,[1] a city of ..., subject to the King of Cambay.[2] After we had watered we went to the fort of Chaul, in which fort we had news that the Governor was about to go to the Straits of Suez with the fleet to burn the galleys. So I at once boarded a small boat in company with a *fidalgo* called Zuan Figera, and we went to Goa, always sailing along the coast, and we went to Cannanore, Bhatkal, Calicut[3] and all those places, and then we came to Goa. And we did not find the Governor there because he had left with the fleet. Then the governors of the said city, together with the Captain, paid me the greatest honour and gave me a horse, and themselves in my company, showed me the whole city without and within, so I saw it all with the greatest pleasure. The next day they gave me a foist to go to Cochin, where the ships were being loaded with spices to go to Portugal, for I intended to depart.

So we arrived in the said city of Cochin in the middle of January 1540,[4] and the Vice-governor, who was the Vedor de Fazenda, did me great honour and gave me a good and large chamber in the King's ship, and four barrels of water and other supplies. And because there was urgency, he was not able to give me supplies of food so suddenly; but the captain of the said ship promised to provide for my consumption. Then I bought a supply from a *fidalgo* who had been about to go to Portugal and then decided again not to go. So he had everything in that provision, and I bought it for 20{0} ducats; thus, I found everything ready and on the 28 January we left Cochin with the said ship, captain Francesco de Sosa, Portuguese.

And to go back to tell of the isle of Hormuz, it is very small and dry, without trees. The island has no more than one city, which city stands by the sea towards Persia. Thus, in the said city there is no water to drink, so all the water comes in boats from the mainland, and they put it in the houses in pitchers and jars. So, in the said city, no fruits grow, nor anything to eat, but everything comes from outside, that is Persia, Basra and India. Hormuz catches many fish; wine is dear, that which comes from India and that which comes from Portugal.

---

1 Also now known as Somnath. On the Kathiawar peninsula west of Diu.

2 The Sultan of Gujarat.

3 Bhatkal, Cannanore and Calicut (in that order) are on the coast to the south of Goa, and would not have been passed approaching Goa from the north. Membré could have visited them on the way from Goa to Cochin. Later he does place Cannanore near Cochin.

4 1541 in modern terms. Cf. p. 1 n. 1 above.

The city is small; it seemed to me to have 2,000 hearths in number, and the fort is very small. It is adjacent to the city, with one part next to the city and one part in the sea, and it has much artillery and the houses are around it. Inside it has a large water citadel. In the said city lives the King of Hormuz who every year pays 300 tumans to the Sophy and 4,000 ducats to the King of Portugal. For, the said King is a Moor, wears the Sophy's cap and speaks Persian. All the people of the city are Moors and a few Portuguese. In the said city they make a very great traffic of merchandise, for merchants of all the world are found there, and sometimes there is scarcity of provisions, and sometimes great abundance. Ships come to the said city of Hormuz from everywhere, that is, from Basra, from India and from the Straits of Mecca. For great business is done in divers merchandise. The money of the said city is a little doubled elongated piece of silver, with the legend of the King on it, which they call *lārī* and *tanka*; and 7 of them are worth one ducat of gold; similarly there is copper money. The said King has a vizier, who also wears the cap of the Sophy.

Chaul is entered by a river, and on the left is the fort, which is very small and weak, with artillery beside the said river, and without the fort are a few houses built of wood and mortar. They are very few, and it seemed to me there were 70 or 80 houses. So, a quarter of a league to the north stands a city of black Gentiles, the houses of straw, wood and mud, together with palm trees and gardens. So, in the said city all are Gentiles, half-blacks wearing clothes, with white cloths on their heads and other naked blacks with a piece of cloth in front. Then, one goes into the city of Bhatkal by a river, and then comes the city of Cannanore, with its fort, near the sea in Calicut, next to the palm trees by the sea. Goa is entered by a river and a kind of island is formed with another river. So, the said city is not surrounded by a wall; and the fortress stands at the entrance, and the houses built of stone, which are good houses, a matter of 1,200 hearths. And at the mouth of the river there is a narrow opening with artillery. So, where the said river is entered on the left is where the ships go to water, for there is a level place which gives good water, since the artillery of the said fort does not reach the said water.[1] So, from Chaul to Cochin are Gentiles, and on the shore of the sea infinite forests of palms, which give the great nuts of India, which are called *coco*. So, the said blacks are always chewing the leaf of a certain tree, which they call *betel*; and it burns the mouth and makes it red. So all the said Gentile blacks go thus chewing all day, both men and women. The women go dressed in a loose shift, and the men naked.

In Cochin the spices are loaded, for there they load the ships. In Cochin there was a matter of 800 houses and a weak fort. Thus, all the forts of India are very weak, except that of Diu, which is very strong. In Cochin there are

---

1 The passage is awkard, but the point would seem to be that the watering place was out of the range of the guns at Goa town and had to have its own provision of artillery.

four elephants, which they use to move full barrels and to move great pieces of wood, of which great ships are made. These elephants understand everything, like a man, but they cannot speak. One of the blacks rides upon the neck of the elephant with a little spear, and talks to it and it understands what he says to it, and moves most skilfully. Fair, great ships are made in Cochin, and galleys, because they have good timber. I have seen about 12 fair galleys in Goa, beside those which the Governor had with him in the fleet. The blacks eat rice without bread, and fishes. Few eat bread or meat. They eat very many nuts, that is, *cocos*. The palm, that is the tree which gives the great nuts of India which they call *coco*, gives various products, that is, oil, vinegar, honey, sugar, wine, cotton, water, matting, and those nuts which are good to eat. It gives fine milk; it gives ship's cordage, called *coir*, and on the leaves they write their letters; they make ships of its wood, and sails. So, from that tree a ship is produced with its supplies for living. In the ships which are made in India they do not put nails in the timbers, but only wood, together with the twine of the said palm tree, except for the ships of the King of Portugal.

I have seen the King of Cochin come riding on an elephant, naked, with a red bonnet and a little piece of cloth in front, in company with 30 or 40 blacks on foot, with their swords and shields. Their swords are of a different form from ours, in such a way that we cannot grip them. I wished to handle one of their swords, and I was unable to get my hand into the grip, it was so tight.[1] And they use them night and day in a way which I cannot convey.

And in the said town of Cochin I found a Venetian jeweller, who was called Messer Piero, who had been married in the city of Venice. He knew me from before, being in Damascus, and for that reason gave me good company. And he gave me many beautiful things as presents, and he gave me certain jewels set in rings, to deliver to a correspondent of his in Lisbon, called Vicenzo Viega, Captain Major of Flanders. In this I promised to serve him.

So we set out from that city of Cochin, as I have already said, on 23 January 1540.[2] And we set out for Portugal, on the way passing many islands which were near Cochin.[3] We met with many calms. Then we sailed for two months and reached the latitude of 34 1/2 which is that of the Cape of Good Hope. In such a way that we could not see land and did not know where we were. So we remained in the said place, with sails reefed, without throwing iron or anchor in the sea; rather, they left the ship in the sea like a pumpkin. So, during the time

---

1 Membré is probably referring to the type of sword known as a gauntlet sword, which was chiefly used in western India and which has a enclosed bar-grip at right angles to the blade. They are usually much too small for the normal European hand.

2 i.e. 1541. Above the date is given as 28 January.

3 The Maldives or Laccadives.

that we remained with sails reefed, there were so many storms, so much wind, such cold and such seas that certainly not one of us thought he would escape, although the wind was in favour of our goal. But because they could not sail safely without seeing or recognizing land, we were forced to stay and wait on the weather. Although, if they had known where they were, with such weather we could have reached Portugal within a month. So, in such torments, after 10 or 12 days had passed, we saw land, for the waters in those parts run like rivers. So, after land had been sighted in 34 degrees, it was known where we were, and then with many labours and prayers we passed the Cape of Good Hope, and after we had passed the said cape we always had fair weather, that is, the wind abaft, until 26 degrees latitude. We sought to make the island of St. Helena to water, but we could not discover it. So we went along, and when we were at 5 degrees latitude, so that there were no more degrees to be found below the line, that is the tropic, there came such rains that the ship was not far from being sent to the bottom from so much water. But if that rain had not fallen we would all have died of thirst. For, in the said ship, although it was very large, there were nevertheless about 400 souls, between blacks and Portuguese. Thus everyone cooked soup day and night; otherwise they would not have been able to live. One lives on rice, salt meat and fresh fish which are caught on the ship every day. So, all those who had something of their own, that is, the rich, used to buy many fine things to eat from India, conserves, chickens, capons, wethers, pigs and many fine things. But those who were poor for the most part died. Thus from the line, where there are no more degrees of latitude, up to 20 degrees, more than 40 Portuguese and 200 blacks died of fever and their gums; for their gums swelled and they were unable to chew bread or biscuit and there was no escape from death. And it was very hot. So I too began to fall ill and such disease came over me, that is, fever, the gums and paralysis, with the sinews drawn tight, that I thought to myself that rather than living it was necessary to make my testament and recommend my soul to God. Then a flux of blood came over me and my mouth and tongue grew so large that I could not speak, so that all the Portuguese were waiting from hour to hour for me to die, so they could throw me into the sea. The Lord God wished to succour me, for on the day I was about to die we sighted land, that is the island of Drizera.[1] So we went with the ship and they somehow disembarked me on to the land, for I could feel nothing. And there were those few jewels which the said Messer Piero of Cochin had given me because they were banned and contraband. And so, as I was disembarked on land, the watch had found them, for the Moors I was bringing with me were carrying them in a little box with me, they knowing nothing about it. So they were taken. Then we stayed on the said island for 20 days, if I am not mistaken, and I recovered myself a little. And we departed in

1 Terçeira in the Azores.

that same ship and came to the Most Honourable King of Portugal's Lisbon in the month of August, on the 19th, of 1541.

APPENDIX

Letters from the Persian Court

The Persian chronicles and other sources of Ṭahmāsp's reign mention a number of the events which Membré himself describes as occuring during his stay at Court, but they are silent about his mission. The chroniclers of the period say very little about relations with European states, and in this case, since the mission produced no result, the episode was not of great importance. For the Persian reaction we do, however, have the evidence of two letters in Persian addressed to the Doge Andrea Gritti which were brought back by Membré and which are still preserved in the archives of Venice. Gritti had died before Membré left Cyprus and been replaced by Pietro Lando, but the letter Membré took to Persia was evidently in his name.

Formally both documents are letters rather than decrees, and one of the features of the letters issued by the Safavid chancery, known also in other Islamic states, is that they do not carry the date on which they were issued. No. 2 reveals that the Shah had heard reliable news of the negotiations for peace being conducted between .(i.Venice: seeks peace with Turkey; and the Sublime Ṗorte, which, according to Membré's account, happened in May or June 1540. No. 1 was evidently issued earlier, at the time when the Shah was planning to send his own envoy to Venice with Membré. Though at points the wording of the two documents is virtually the same and passages have been recycled from the first to the second, the two letters differ in their narrative standpoint. In No. 1 the Shah is throughout referred to in the third person while in No. 2 the Royal We occurs on several occasions. Differences in the seals and Persian notes on the backs also indicate that the letters are not of the same type; The first, though representing Royal policy, was in fact a letter of the Minister Qāḍī-yi Jahān, whose large seal appears on its back. It appears that it entered the Venetian archives as such. Possibly Ṭahmāsp wished to distance himself a little from a conciliatory policy towards non-Muslims at first, but when they could justifiably be accused of double-dealing was willing to speak in propria persona.

The letters are in the elaborate style favoured by Persian scribes for courtly communications for many centuries, replete with parallelisms, rhymes, allusive periphrases, metaphors and bombast. It stands in marked contrast to Membré's own style. Translation, a desperate undertaking in such cases, has been attempted below, but a summary and discussion of the contents may be more useful. The main text of both letters starts with the address to the Doge, respectful enough, except for the prayers for the conversion of the infidel addressee, a point picked up again at the end of the second letter. This, however, was conventional when addressing the unbeliever. Though even Qāḍī-yi Jahān's letter is likely to have been handed over considerably later, both begin with Membré's first audience with the Shah at Marand, for which No. 2 gives a precise date, to be read 5 Rabī‘ I 946/21 July 1539. This contradicts Membré himself, who places his own arrival at court in August.

In No. 1 Qāḍī-yi Jahān describes the delivery and reading of the letter from Venice, the Shah's enquiries from Membré, the welcome he gave to the news of the League of the four powers, his exposition of the situation to his brothers and the rest of the court, and his announcement that the time was right for a campaign to crush the Turks and for the opening of relations with the League. The representation of all this as taking place at the one audience is evidently a fiction and Membré himself (p. 22) is no doubt right in giving a more limited account of the progress made on that occasion. The self-congratulatory hyperbole was standard in the diplomatic correspondence of Persian rulers, and is made necessary more by the demands of the writers' positions in their own societies than by any expectation that it would be taken seriously by the recipients. Nevertheless, the letter does convey that Ṭahmāsp viewed the idea of co-operation with the League with favour, and was prepared to pursue negotiations, though there is no reason to think that he took any serious steps towards mounting the devastating invasion described with such vigour in the letter. Towards the end the affairs of Mīkā'īl Beg, as the Cypriot merchant has become, are considered. His courage and enterprise in carrying out his dangerous mission had naturally impressed the Shah, and he was duly rewarded. Brief reference is then made to a second audience in which the Shāh emphasised, somewhat ambiguously, that if the League's intention was to destroy the enemies of religion they would certainly achieve their desires. This second audience is no doubt that mentioned briefly in the Relazione (p. 27) and described more fully in Membré's despatches.

No. 2, Ṭahmāsp's own letter to Gritti, begins with a similiar, but shorter, description of Membré's first audience, and the welcome his mission received. Rumours however reached the Shah that the 'famed Sultans', that is the allied European rulers, had sent an envoy to the Ottomans to make peace. In the hope that this news would be contradicted, the Shah postponed receiving Membré again. The implication is that he was expecting to grant him a final audience in which he would be given formal leave to depart. However, the news of the peace negotiations was confirmed beyond doubt, and Membré was given permission to leave the court (presumably without meeting the Shah again). He was to report the reasons why the Safavid army had not moved against Turkey, and bring home the point that there was no fault on Ṭahmāsp's part. Nevertheless, soon, if God willed, at the right moment the Persian army would attack and destroy the Turks, and the European powers would be well advised to make ready for the opportunity that would then be presented to them.

The question of Membré's departure from the court and that of Ṭahmāsp's attitude to the alliance have been discussed in the Introduction (pp. xxi-xxiii). The Shah's letter agrees with the account of the Relazione, rather than the more dramatic version given in the despatches. Although Venice's peace negotiations marked the collapse of the Holy League as such, it is unlikely that they were really misunderstood in Persia as applying to all four of the allied powers. From Membré's despatches it is clear that he had discussed the league's forces in detail. Von Palombini also quotes a conversation he had with Ghāzī Khān Takkalū shortly before his departure in which he was told that Sulaimān had rejected the peace offers of Venice because he was threatened with an Austrian attack, which would be supported by Charles V, and because he was afraid of being betrayed by Venice. Possibly it was Ghāzī Khān's knowledge of Western affairs that in some way enabled him to assist Membré to leave..i).Venice: seeks peace with Turkey;

Translations

1. From Qāḍī-yi Jahān to Andrea Gritti.

He is God, praise to him.

May the causes of the greatness and dominion and the effects of the grandeur and power of Your Highness, layer of the foundations of justice and beneficence, propagator of the ways of security and tranquillity, destroyer of the bases of injustice and oppression, refuter of the arguments of falsity amongst all people, Khaqan of famed Khaqans - may God on High illuminate your heart with the light of faith - Sultan of powerful Sultans, heroic one in greatness, command, power, justice, rule, strength, equity, honour and glorification, Andrea Gritti, Doge of Venice - may God on High expand your breast with the joy of the purification of religion - moment by moment continue and ascend, and the star of eternal fortune, and the luminary of glorification in both worlds - after acceptance of the felicity of Islam through the grace of divine bounty - instant by instant progress and wax.

To continue, it is submitted to your judgement, the resolver of difficulties, that: On the date of the month of Rabīʻ al-Avval of the year nine hundred and forty six, in the neighbourhood of the district of Marand among the dependencies of the Seat of Sovereignty, Tabriz, where was the encampment of the pavilions of the greatness and glory, the pitching-place of the tents of the sovereignty and glorification of His Fortunate, Exalted, Royal, Kingly Majesty - may God make his kingship and sovereignty eternal, and fill the worlds with his goodness and beneficence - His Excellency of fortunate works, the scion of great commanders, Mīkā'īl Beg - may his success endure - having been, under the direction of the caravan-leader of True Guidance, privileged and distinguished with the honour of kissing the threshold - the abode of the angels - of the slaves of the court which resembles the heavenly throne, that refuge of the lote-tree of Paradise, which is the qibla of those with needs, the kaʻba of those with prayers to ask, delivered to the most noble and exalted perusal the charming letters of your honourable servants. And His Fortunate Exalted Majesty - may God make his kingship and sovereignty eternal, and fill the worlds with his goodness and beneficence - after perusal and contemplation, enquiring from the aforementioned about the news and affairs of those parts, made investigation; and in the paradisiac assembly the aforementioned, in the way that is the manner of possessors of eloquence, the custom of men of powers of speech and perception, expounded the nature of the situation truly; and the luminous mind and brilliant, world-adorning judgement of His Exalted Majesty, the Khaqan, from moment to moment became [more] expansive and joyful from his joy-mingled expressions, his happiness-rousing words. So much so that, from the moment the sun rose until time of sunset, he gave his attention to his wonderful effusions and strange expressions by way of enquiring about the course of affairs in those parts, in particular the happy union of the famous Sultans and powerful Khaqans of those regions, which had not previously occurred; and His Fortunate Royal Majesty expounded in his own precious person what of this account of affairs received the form of inscription on the mirror of his soul, effulgent as the sun, to his world-conquering, angelic-throned sons, his kingdom-adorning, country-capturing brothers, his solar-bannered, wisely-planning commanders, his joyful-hearted, brilliant-souled chancellors, his high-ranking, Mercury-like ministers, the deputies of the pavilion of glory, the chamberlains of the gates of eternity and grandeur, the remainder of the pillars of the sovereignty which is ordered like the heavens and the rest of the notables of the Sultanate which will endure to eternity; and with ruby-bearing, pearl-scattering words he declared, 'Now that those four famed monarchs have become united it is time that, our royal, victory-attended banners too, having, with the heaven-assisted armies also turned toward those climes, and having, with the crashing strokes of the shining sword and the thunder of fire-dealing cannon and gun, brought ruin upon the evil days of the luckless forces of the ill-starred and heretical Rūmīs, we should bring their conquered kingdoms into the possession of the servants of the exalted threshold, and purify the world of the filth of their existence; and bring to manifestation with regard to those great, high-standing governors what is the perfection of unstinted Royal kindness and limitless kingly mercy; and that, the road of love and friendship being trod, the gates of correspondence and communication should be open, so that persons going to and fro may do so without disturbance or hardship and there be none to prevent or hinder them.' And after explanation of the matter so that His fortunate, most exalted Majesty had full information about the bewilderment, disturbance and difficulty on the road in Rum and the other things which had befallen the said Mīkā'īl Beg, greatly astonished at his firmness, courage, sincerity and nobility, he bestowed upon him kindnesses and favours of many sorts and repeatedly rendered him glorious and proud with royal robes of honour, and at his return to the foot of the throne, the place of the Caliphate, insistently stated: if their attention to destroying and ruining the foundations of the enemies of religion and good fortune also displays itself, it is certain that aims and ambitions will turn out in accordance with desires. No more. May the shade of [your] glory and fortune be eternal and enduring over the heads of the people of the world.

2. From Shāh Ṭahmāsp to Andrea Gritti.

He is the King of Kingship, the Exalted.

O Muḥammad, O ʻAlī.

May the causes of the greatness and dominion and the effects of the grandeur and power of the Khaqan of famed Khaqans - may God on High illuminate his heart with the light of faith - Sultan of powerful Sultans, heroic one in lordship, command, dignity, grandeur and gravity, Andrea, Doge of Venice, Khān - may God on High expand his breast with the joy of the purification of religion - moment by moment continue and ascend, and the star of eternal fortune - after acceptance of the felicity of Islam through the grace of divine bounty - instant by instant progress and wax.

To continue, it is communicated that: On the date of 5 Rabīʻ al-Avval of the year nine hundred and forty six, he whose acts are attended by felicity, the scion of amirs, Mīkā'īl Beg - may his felicity endure - having become privileged and distinguished with the honour of kissing the threshold - the abode of the angels - of the slaves of the court which resembles the heavenly throne, that refuge of the lote-tree of Paradise, which is the qibla of those with needs, the kaʻba of those with prayers to ask, delivered to the most noble and exalted perusal their charming letters and explained the particulars and true nature of affairs of those parts as they are, in the way they deserve, especially the happy union of those famed Sultans which has at this juncture been concerted to ruin and destroy the evildoers.

To the perfume-diffusing mind, abundant as the ocean, it so occurred that no opportunity better than this would present itself for us, at the time of the alliancei.Holy League; of those powerful Khaqans, our royal, victory-attended banners having, with the heaven-assisted armies also turned toward those climes, and having, with the strokes of the shining sword and the thunder of fire-dealing cannon and gun, brought ruin upon the evil days of the luckless forces of the ill-starred Rūmīs, to bring their conquered kingdoms into the possession of the servants of the exalted threshold, and purify the world of the filth of their existence; and to bring to manifestation with regard to those great, high-standing governors what would be the perfection of the unstinted Royal kindness and the limitless Kingly mercy; and, the road of love and friendship being trod, for the gates of communication and correspondence henceforth to be open, so that, persons going to and fro doing so without disturbance or hardship, there be none to prevent or hinder them. When, from mouths and tongues it was repeatedly heard that those famed Sultans had at this juncture sent one on an embassy to the territory of the ill-starred Rūmīs and that, determined in the intention of making peace and deleting the former claims and the contents of the associated letters which at this juncture they had sent with Mīkā'īl Beg, they had not remained fixed and firm in their promises.

The hearing of these reports indicated their untrustworthiness, and for this reason the coming of the aforementioned Mīkā'īl Beg to the Presence in the Royal camp was till now delayed, to see if perhaps the said news had no basis. Still, when repeatedly and on numerous occasions confirmation of it attained manifestation from possessors of good credit, its truth became apparent to the Majestic Royal mind. Having given the aforementioned leave to depart, he has been sent to the [Doge's] Presence so that, having investigated the said reports he should bring the truth about the circumstances and activities of these parts to their hearing and at this juncture submit to that quarter the reason for the pausing of the Royal, victory-attended banners, so that it may be clear to their judgement that from this side there has been, and will be, no failure.

And soon, if the One Glorious God wills, at the moment of opportunity, whether they are in alliance or they are not, by the help of the stainless Imams - God's blessings upon them all - the victory-attended banners, in glory, strength and power, having turned to that quarter, destruction will be brought upon their [the Turks'] treacherous days. If they [the Doge and his allies] too, having become informed of the situation, are organized and prepared to make ready the means for that, it will be best and most appropriate.

Peace be upon him who follows True Guidance.

Bibliographical Note

The text of No. 2 was first published in 1910 by Bonelli, who gave an Italian translation. No. 1, which had been misleadingly catalogued in the archives, had to wait until 1968 when it was made the subject of an article by G-R. Scarcia, which illustrated the document and provided a transcription and an Italian translation. The following year photographs and transcriptions of both appeared in the Italian edition of Membré's Relazione. Italian translations are given in the introduction to the same work (pp. xliii-v, lix-lx). Photographs, accompanied by (better) texts in Arabic script and translations into German, have also been published in the name of L. Fekete from materials left by him.

BIOGRAPHICAL NOTES

ʻAbdallāh Khān (Ustājlū). Son of Qarā Khān Ustājlū and nephew of Shāh Ismāʻīl's important amir Khān Muḥammad Ustājlū. His mother was one of Shāh Ismāʻīl's sisters and he himself married one of Ṭahmāsp's sisters (see below, under Ṭahmāsp, Sisters of). During 1526-1529 the Ustājlū were driven into exile by the opposition of other Qizilbāsh tribes. ʻAbdallāh Khān's royal blood may have given him some protection. Soon afterwards he became one of the Shah's leading commanders. In autumn 1550 he was appointed Governor of Shīrvān, a position he retained until his death in 1566. Anthony Jenkinson, the representative of the English Muscovy Company, whom he entertained in 1562, has left a fine description.

Abū Bakr. Caliph (AD 632-634). According to the Sunni Muslims, chosen, after the Prophet Muḥammad's death, to be the leader of the Muslim community, that is, to be Caliph. Regarded by the Shi'ites as usurping the position which rightfully belonged to ʻAlī and, particularly in the early Safavid period, as Membré vividly describes it, constantly cursed, together with the two succeeding Caliphs, ʻUmar and ʻUthmān, by the *tabarrā'īs* who attended upon the Shah and the Qizilbāsh grandees.

ʻAlī. Caliph (656-661). The cousin of the prophet Muḥammad, husband of his only daughter Fāṭima and father of his grandsons Ḥasan and Ḥusain. Seen by the Sunnis as the fourth and last of the 'rightly-guided' Caliphs who led the Muslim community after Muḥammad's death. In Shīʻi eyes he should have been Muḥammad's immediate successor and was unjustly excluded. For the twelver Shīʻa he is the first of the twelve Imams. The epithet *murtaḍā*, 'approved of (by God)', is particularly his. The Safavid family claimed to be descendants of ʻAlī, and hence bore the title Sayyid.

Alqāṣ Mīrzā. Son of Shāh Ismāʻīl, half-brother of Ṭahmāsp, and closest to him in age, for he was born in March 1516. He had participated in the campaign to reduce Shīrvān alluded to by Membré, which took place in 1538, and he was made governor of the province, though at first he was provided with a *lala*, or guardian. Some years on, and now in full control of his province, he showed signs of disloyalty and he later fled to Turkey. He participated in the Ottoman invasion of Persia in 1548, but fell into Persian captivity. Ṭahmāsp himself, who certainly ought to have known, wrote that he had his brother sent to the prison-fortress of Alamūt, adding that after a few days he was thrown to his death from it, an act of private vengeance by some people whose father he had killed. Other contemporary sources locate the incident at another castle, Qahqaha in Adharbaijan. Inevitably, there were those who suggested that the Shah was behind his brother's death. It is said to have occurred in March-April 1550.

Arab Sayyid of Baghdad. The owner of the house in Tabriz noticed by Membré may be Sayyid Muḥammad Kamūna. His father, who had the same name, won Shāh Ismā'īl's approval when the latter conquered Baghdad and Arab Iraq. The family were leading Sayyids from Najaf in the south of Iraq.

Bahrām Mīrzā. Full brother of Ṭahmāsp. The Prince was born in September 1517, and was thus twenty two or three at the time of Membré's visit. The plot to substitute him for Ṭahmāsp is not mentioned elsewhere; Persian sources which mention the banishment of Tājlū Begum (q.v.) do not implicate him. Both before and after the disgrace of his mother Bahrām was trusted with important military commands and governorships, and, in contrast to Sām and Alqāṣ, he never betrayed Ṭahmāsp, though reports that he was in rebellion were current on at least one occasion later.

His brother Sām's notice of him, written shortly after his death at thirty two in October 1549 agrees with Membré in noting the gusto with which Bahrām lived and speaks of his exceptional talents: he was an excellent calligrapher in *nasta'līq* script and skilled at drawing, poetry and riddles. He was also a patron of literature and painting. At times he turned to music and himself played. Membré's appears to be the only account of his heroic drinking habits, but his addiction to opium was notorious. The most detailed account of the fever that killed him, coming from one of the physicians present, describes the steps taken to reduce his intake of opium and other drugs.

Bairām Beg Chāvushlū. This seems a likely interpretation of Membré's Pairam Pecchevasli, though no such person appears recognisably in the chronicles. The Chāvushlū were a clan of the Ustājlū.

Bāshī āchuq. Turkish *bāshı-āchuk*, meaning bare-headed. Title applied to the Kings of the Georgian kingdom of Imeretia, the capital of which was Kutaisi. *Bāshī-āchuq* appears to be the form favoured by the Persians, while the Ottomans often used the alternative *āchuq-bāsh*. At the time of Membré's visit the King was Bagrat III (1510-1548).

Benedetti, Bernardo. A man of this name is mentioned as enjoying revenues estimated at 500 ducats in a list of the Lords of the Manor of Cyprus reproduced by de Mas Latrie (iii, p. 500). The editor believed the document to come from before 1500; if so this man may be Membré's patron's father or grandfather.

Dadian, King of Mingrelia. Dadian(i) is not a personal name but the title by which the Georgian Princes of Mingrelia were known.

Emperor, The. Charles V of Spain, Holy Roman Emperor 1519-1558.

Farrukhzād Beg. (Text: Furgusat pech) The chief of the *yasāvuls*, according to Membré. It is probable that this was Farrukhzād Beg Qarādāghlū. He is first mentioned in Persian sources in 1555, when he was sent as ambassador to Turkey in the course of the peace negotiations which led to the treaty of Amasia. The sources describe his position at court differently, but this may reflect a change in terminology rather than any real conflict. Ṭahmāsp refers to Farrukhzād Beg as Īshīk-āqāsī, while some of the other sources have Īshīk-āqāsī-bāshī. (See Glossary: *īshīk-āqāsī*) On the other hand, Khwurshāh b. Qubād, who represented the Niẓāmshāh of the Deccan at Ṭahmāsp's court a few years after Membré's visit, and who, like him, must have known the personnel of the court, agrees with his fellow-envoy, for he calls Farrukhzād Beg Yasāvul-bāshī, chief *yasāvul*. Farrukhzād Beg died in 1574-1575 and the notice of his death in the *Khulāṣat al-Tavārīkh* indicates that he had then been Īshīk-āqāsī bāshī of the Dīvān for some years.

Ghāzī Khān (Takkalū). 'A deceitful, devilish, cheating, lying wretch.' So Shāh Ṭahmāsp, writing years after he had had him put to death. Membré's account of Ghāzī Khān's appearance at court is confirmed by the Persian chronicles, which credit him with a following of 5,000 or 6,000 cavalry. What details we have of his chequered career give the impression of an unusually persuasive, energetic and capable character but one whose ultimate aims are difficult to perceive. It is interesting that he played an important part in arranging for Membré to be permitted to leave Ṭahmāsp's court at a time when he had only just returned to Safavid allegiance after years of disloyalty.

The major part of the Takkalū tribe were incorporated into the Qizilbāsh forces in Iran later than most other such groups. A large body of them left south-western Anatolia in the course of the revolt against the Ottoman government led by Shāh qulī. They took refuge in Iran in 1511, having acquired a reputation for violence. Their initial leaders were put to death by Shāh Ismā'īl, but they emerged as one of the most important of the Qizilbāsh tribes. Towards the end of Shāh Ismā'īl's reign Ghāzī Khān's father, Chirkīn

('Filthy') Ḥasan, had been executed by the current favourite, Dīv Sulṭān Rūmlū, for failing to keep discipline among his forces on campaign in Georgia. In the time of Ṭahmāsp, Ghāzī Khān rose from being on the staff of, perhaps Keeper of, the Royal Wardrobe to himself become an important commander. In 1530, when Bahrām Mīrzā was left at Herat as Governor of Khurasan, he was appointed the Prince's *lala*. While at Herat they faced a cruel siege by the Uzbeks which lasted a year and a half. When Ṭahmāsp finally arrived with his army in winter 1533-1534 Ghāzī Khān declared that his men should be relieved. The Governorship of Khuraṣan was given to Sām Mīrzā. Ghāzī Khān was censured for the way he and his followers had treated the inhabitants of Herat.

However, thanks to being in Khurasan, he had not been directly involved in the quarrelling among the Qizilbāsh tribes at court which had led to the massacre of the Takkalū in summer 1531. This 'Takkalū disaster' must nevertheless have been on his mind, for at Herat Ṭahmāsp, as he himself tells us, had been persuaded to swear that he would not kill Ghāzī Khān unless he came against him in armed rebellion. (The oath was a wise precaution: Ḥusain Khān Shāmlū was to be executed on suspicion of intending to join the Ottomans.) Ghāzī Khān was with the Safavid army as the Shah returned westward to face Sulṭān Sulaimān, who had been encouraged to invade by another Takkalū, the renegade Ulāma. Ghāzī Khān deserted Shāh Ṭahmāsp at this point. Not only did he he join the Ottomans, but he also informed them that Sām Mīrzā (q.v.) had abandoned Herat and was in rebellion. Sulaimān was glad for the opportunity to acknowledge Sām, *in absentia*, as his son and promise that the throne of Persia would be his. The reasons for Ghāzī Khān's return to Safavid allegiance, the occasion observed by Membré, are not known, but presumably the Ottoman Empire failed to supply him and his following with a congenial niche. Ṭahmāsp gave him a territory or fief (*ulkā*) to the south of Shīrvān, and even appointed him *lala* to Alqāṣ Mīrzā, but early in 1545 Alqāṣ was ordered to execute him, persistent treachery and disloyalty being given as the reason.

Goa, Governor of. The term is commonly used, as here, to refer to the Governor of Portuguese India, who, from 1540-1542, and therefore at the time of Membré's visit, was Estavão da Gama, son of Vasco da Gama. The expedition to the Red Sea to burn the Ottoman galleys at Suez had set off on 1 January 1541. It reached Suez but failed in its main objective as the enemy was present in force.

Gritti, Andrea. Doge of Venice from 1523 until his death on 28 December 1538. The letter taken to Persia was evidently in his name though he had died before Membré was even commissioned to deliver it. Gritti was succeeded by Pietro Lando (1539-1545).

Gūkcha (Gökçe) Sulṭān. Of the Qājār tribe of the Qizilbāsh. Probably the names given by Membré as Cochie sultan and Chiachchich sultan both refer to this same man. He does not seem to be mentioned by the Persian sources among the commanders sent against Ḥājjī Shaikh as stated by Membré, who was not therefore necessarily mistaken. He was certainly at court during Membré's stay, for we know that he went with Bahrām Mīrzā on the minor Kurdish expedition of the previous year, on which Membré himself was present. He is mentioned as a commander later and was *lala* of Prince Ismā'īl Mīrzā. He fell ill and died while on campaign in the region of Astarabad in 1555.

Ḥājjī Shaikh, Kurd. The expedition against the Kurd Ḥājjī Shaikh is mentioned in the Persian chronicles, and their lists of the commanders contain several names in common with that of Membré: 'Abdallāh Khān Ustājlū, Shāh qulī Khalīfah, Keeper of the Seal, Ghāzī Khān Takkalū. The terrain was difficult and the Persian army met little success. The chronicles fail to tell us where the theatre of operations was. It has been plausibly suggested that the campaign was against the Bābān Kurds of Shahrazūr. They had had a chief called Ḥājjī Shaikh, who had rebuffed several Safavid attacks on his territories. However, he had been killed in the winter of 1534-1535 and in 1541 his son Būdāq Beg was chief.

Han Mocassal. This may stand for Khān Muḥaṣṣil. Muḥaṣṣil would mean student, referring to the little boy's studies.

Humāyūn Pādishāh. The Moghul Emperor of India, who had succeeded his father Bābur in December 1530 and who died in 1556. The mission sent to him by Ṭahmāsp does not seem to mentioned elsewhere, and probably came to nothing, for in June 1540 Humāyūn had suffered his second defeat at the hands of Shīr Khān Sūr at the battle of Qanauj, and by the end of the year he was in a precarious position in Sind, faced with the disloyalty of his brothers and others. In 1544 he arrived as a refugee at the court of Ṭahmāsp, and it was the latter's assistance that enabled him to take Qandahar in the next year. From that position he was eventually able to defeat the Afghans and re-establish himself as ruler of North India. The name is spelt Hunus by Membré, but the recognisable Pādshāh makes the identification reasonably secure.

Hormuz, King of. When the Portuguese occupied the island of Hormuz in 1515 they maintained the existing dynasty of Kings of Hormuz as useful subordinates. The King at the time of Membré's visit was known to the

Portuguese as Xargol Xa, for Salghur Shāh. Membré's indications that at such a late date the King was to some extent regarded as a Safavid as well as a Portuguese vassal are noteworthy. Portuguese sources record a fierce dispute between the King and the Captain of Hormuz, Martim Afonso de Melo (q.v.), which must have been in progress when Membré was in the island. Portuguese pressure continued and in 1542 Salghur Shāh was compelled to relinquish his valuable rights in the Customs House at Hormuz, a significant step in the decline of the dynasty. According to do Couto he died in November 1543.

Ḥusain, Imām. Second son of ʻAlī and Muḥammad's daughter Fāṭima, and third Imam of the Shi'ites. His attempt to claim the Caliphate led to his death at the hands of the troops of the Umayyad government at Karbalā in southern Iraq on 10 Muḥarram 61/10 October 680. His martyrdom is commemorated each year by the Shi'ites in the Muḥarram ceremonies which culminate on the 10th, *ʻĀshūrā'*.

Kūpik-qirān (Köpek-qıran). Meaning, as Membré says, *mazzacani* 'dog-slayer'. Turkish: *köpek* dog, *qırmak* to break, destroy, kill. Presumably a nickname-like title; Shāh Ismāʻīl had a weakness for nicknames. Kūpik-kirān is mentioned by Ṭahmāsp as one of the commanders in his campaign in the Van region in 1534-1535. The *Takmilat al-Akhbār*, the author of which used Ṭahmāsp's memoir but was also present on the campaign, provides his real name, Ḥusain ʻAlī Beg Qājār. A miniature portrait, preserved in Istanbul, shows him carrying the baton of a *yasāvul*, and confirms the accuracy of Membré's description of his portly figure.

Kurdish Lord. The Persian histories identify the Kurdish leader against whom Bahrām Mīrzā's campaign was directed as Sulṭān ʻAlī Batanlīj (or Ghanlīj, or Tabanlīj?). He is associated with the district of Bāna, in the north of present-day Persian Kurdistan. The histories also mention, though less fully than Membré, the punishment of the Qizilbāsh who had flouted the Shah's orders on this occasion.

Lavand Beg, King of Georgia. Levan II, of the Georgian kingdom of Kakheti (1520-1574). Membré gives the name as Leompech and Levan comes from Latin Leo but in Persian the form Lavand was normally used, no doubt because of the existence of a Persian homophone meaning 'libertine, debauched young man'.

Luarsab, King of Gori. Luarsab I, of the Georgian kingdom of Kartli (1535-1558).

Mahdī, The. For the Twelver Shi'ites the twelfth and last of the Imams. He is believed to have disappeared at Samarra as an infant in 260/874 but to be alive and present in the world. Even in his absence no other has a true right to rule and the community awaits his reappearance to usher in a period of just rule preparatory to the end of the world. To indicate their hopes of his return, Shi'ite communities sometimes maintained a horse, ready for him to ride whenever he chose to reveal himself. The provision of a bride for the Mahdī from the Safavid Royal Family is a practice of a similar nature, though apparently confined to the reign of Ṭahmāsp. Expectations of the Mahdī's imminent reappearance were current in Persia in the mid-sixteenth century and helped shape Ṭahmāsp's beliefs and policies.

Mantashā Sulṭān. Of the Shaikhlū clan of the Ustājlū tribe. He is first mentioned in the chronicles for killing Shāh Ismā'īl's brother Sulaimān Mīrzā. During Ismā'īl's absence on campaign in Khurāsān in 1513, Sulaimān had begun an ill-organized rebellion by attempting to capture Tabriz. Mantashā was a simple *qūrchī* at the time; his daring action was evidently approved. In the next year he fought among the *qūrchīs* at the battle of Chāldirān, where his elder brother the Qūrchībāshī Sārū Pīra was among the numerous Safavid casualties. In the 'Ustājlū war' Mantashā appears as one of the Ustājlū amirs who in 1526, after battles with the Shah's army, took refuge in Gīlān. The Ustājlū were reconciled with Ṭahmāsp in 1529 and Mantashā became one of the chief amirs. He died suddenly in 1545 in Nakhjawān which was his *ulkā* or 'fief'. Membré's mention of his building operations in the same town implies that he had already been given the *ulkā* of Nakhjawān by 1539.

Melo, Martin Afonso de. Martim Afonso de Melo Juzarte acted as Captain of Hormuz in an interim capacity in 1539-1540 and served a normal three-year term as Captain there from 1541-1544. According to the information of Correa, at the end of the first of these two periods of office he arrived in Goa at the end of 1540, shortly before the Portuguese Governor Da Gama set out on his expedition to the Red Sea. He must then have left Hormuz very soon after Membré's departure, and made a swifter passage, to reach Goa in advance of Membré.

Mosto, Domenigo da. The son of Niccolo. Lieutenant of Cyprus 1536-1539. The island was under direct Venetian rule from 1489, and lost to the Turks in 1570.

Nāranjī Sulṭān. The affectation of the colour orange (*nāranjī* in Persian), and perhaps even the name to match, must have been approved by the Shah and attest to the aesthetic interests and sophisticated, even precious, tastes of the latter in his younger days. The chronicles ignore Nāranjī Sulṭān, but Sām Mīrzā gives him a disdainfully witty notice in the *Tuḥfah-i Sāmī*. The son of Yārī Sulṭān, he came from the region of Shahrazūr (which confirms Membré's statement that he was of Kurdish origin). Initially he had been in the retinue of the powerful Amir Kūpik Sulṭān Ustājlū, but, at the time Sām Mīrzā was writing, he had been in Bahrām Mīrzā's service for twenty years. His claims to military prowess remained unsubstantiated. He had received the title Sulṭān because he had been given command of a group called *namad-pūshān*, 'wearers of felt', who used to be in the Royal camp. It is not evident who the *namad-pūshān* were; some unusual Sufi group, perhaps. However, we are told by Sām Mīrzā that they called themselves the army of *riḍā*. (This may refer to the eighth Imam, 'Alī al-Riḍā, or to God's approval, *riḍā*.) Besides commanding this dubious force, Nāranjī Sulṭān composed poetry in Turkish and Persian. Sām Mīrzā finally justifies the length of his notice on the grounds that it is appropriate to its subject's garrulousness.

Portugal, King of. Dom João III, r. 1521-1557.

Qāḍī-yi Jahān. Ṭahmāsp's Chief Minister at the time of Membré's mission, Qāḍī-yi Jahān came from an old family of clerics, the Saifī Sayyids of Qazvin, who claimed descent from the Prophet Muḥammad's grandson Ḥasan, the elder brother of Ḥusain. He was born in 1483. His father had been the chief Qāḍī or judge of Qazvin, and he himself acted as judge there for a time. The very name Qāḍī-yi Jahān, and the usual sources give no other, means 'Judge of the World'. However, some time late in the reign of Ismā'īl he became attached to the court, as an administrator rather than a judge or theologian. He successfully supervised the construction of a canal from the Euphrates to Najaf, the shrine town at the site of the grave of 'Alī, and became one of the ministers of Ismā'īl's vizier Mīrzā Shāh Ḥusain. After the latter's murder in April 1523 Qāḍī-yi Jahān became vizier to the boy prince Ṭahmāsp, who was with his father in the last year or so of the latter's reign.

On Ṭahmāsp's accession Qāḍī-yi Jahān was put in charge of the bureaucracy, though for some years supreme power lay with a succession of Qizilbāsh amirs. Qāḍī-yi Jahān was a partisan of the Ustājlu tribe: one of his daughters was married to the son of Kūpik Sulṭān. When the Ustājlū came under pressure from the other tribes Qāḍī-yi Jahān was dismissed and imprisoned in the castle of Lori on the Georgian border (where Membré entered the Shah's dominions). Freed by 'Abdallāh Khān Ustājlū, Qāḍī-yi Jahān was brought to court but later, like many of the Ustājlū, he took refuge in Gīlān. Here he fell into the hands of an old enemy, Amīra Dubbāj, ruler of Rasht, who held him in prison for ten years. When Amīra Dubbāj himself was ousted and executed, Qāḍī-yi Jahān was able to return to court. There in August 1535 he was again entrusted with administrative affairs, at first jointly, and then, after the fall of the colleague who attempted to discredit him, as sole minister. This was the position when Membré saw him; Ṭahmāsp was now in full control and there was no question of any Qizilbāsh amir acting as Vakīl. In fact, though the literary sources sometimes call Qāḍī-yi Jahān vizier, he is also referred to as Vakīl and that is the title which appears with his name on the back of the letter from him which Membré brought to Venice. Membré himself refers to him as Ṭahmāsp's *governador* and once, it seems, as *governador* and *khalīfa*. The use of the latter term is unexpected.

Qāḍī-yi Jahān remained the Shah's minister for nearly fifteen years. In fact, Ṭahmāsp had sworn that he would never dismiss him and it was not until early in 1549 that, at his own request, he was allowed to retire to Qazvin. He was approaching seventy and his old age and inability to follow the Shah on his travels were the stated reasons for his retirement, though it was also suggested that Ṭahmāsp had begun to enquire too closely into matters which had previously been left to him. Some years later he went to visit the Royal Camp. The Shah, mindful of the provisions of his oath no doubt, was worried that if Qāḍī-yi Jahān asked for the still-vacant position of Vakīl again he could not refuse him. A new Vakīl was hastily appointed, and on his return journey from the camp Qāḍī-yi Jahān died (November 1553).

Qāḍī-yi Jahān is stated by the chroniclers to have been a highly intelligent and learned man and a capable administrator. He was a good calligrapher and prose stylist: the official documents he composed were copied and used as models. His piety is also noted and in particular the respect he had for the descendents of the Prophet and those learned in religious law. Yet it may be that he was not as enthusiastic for the Shī'a religion imposed by the Safavids as might be expected for one in his position. Like many long-established clerical families of Iran the Saifīs of Qazvīn had been unquestioned Sunnis until the end of the fifteenth century. When Shi'ism was imposed by Ismā'īl the alternative to submission was emigration or worse, and the majority submitted. In many cases the choice must have been taken for tactical reasons. The survival of the Safavid state, and the eventual victory of Shi'ism could not have been foreseen, and it must also have been evident that the religion of the militant Qizilbāsh and their early leaders was, if to be regarded as Islamic at all, an extreme heresy quite distinct from the Ithnā 'asharī Shi'ism of the books of law (which eventually prevailed). Most of the Persian *'ulamā* who converted seem to have made the transition smoothly enough; of course, it was not in their interest to preserve a record of their doubts. However, some of the clerics of Qazvīn, including members of the Saifī family, did evidently continue to favour Sunnism. Not long after Qāḍī-yi Jahān's death a number of them were subjected to persecution for that reason, and there is considerable evidence that Ṭahmāsp's minister was sympathetic to their views.

Qarā Khalīfa Shāmlū. The *Khulāṣat al-Tawarikh* mentions Qarā Khalīfa Shāmlū as one of the followers of Bahrām Mīrzā who were sent to accompany the corpse of the Prince to its final resting-place in Mashhad in 1549. Given Membré's information on the various members of the family in Bahrām Mīrzā's service, his Chiamni may be taken to represent the tribal name Shāmlū.

Qūrchībāshī, the. The commander of the Royal Guard, the *qūrchīs*, the main standing corps of the Shah's army at this period (see Glossary). Membré refers to the Qūrchībāshī only by his title, no doubt following the usage of the court, but at the time the post was held by Sivindūk Beg Afshār. This already venerable figure is said to have been one of the 'Sufis of Gilan', that is, to have been with Ismā'īl in Gilan before the original Safavid revolt in 1499. At the time of Membré's visit he had only been Qūrchībāshī for a few years but he still had long to live and eventually died in office aged over 90 in January 1562.

Sām Mīrzā. Son of Shāh Ismā'īl and half-brother of Shāh Ṭahmāsp. Younger than the twenty eight stated by Membré, since he was born, within a few days of Bahrām Mīrzā, in September 1517. He would have been twenty two or twenty three when Membré saw him.

Though Membré provides corroboration of the fact, he does not make it clear whether he was aware that Sām Mīrzā was in disgrace. That is why Ṭahmāsp did not give him any power. At the end of 1521, near the end of his father's life and when he himself was four, Sām had been appointed Governor of Khurasan. He succeeded Ṭahmāsp, who had received the appointment at an even earlier age. The effective Governor was of course the *lala*, Dūrmīsh Khān Shāmlū, and subsequently Dūrmīsh's brother Ḥusain Khān, whose daughter was at some stage married to Sām Mīrzā. (The brothers were sons of 'Abdī Beg Shāmlū by a sister of Shāh Ismā'īl.) Under Uzbek pressure and receiving little support from the court, in 1529 Ḥusain Khān negotiated a safe withdrawal and abandoned Herat to the Uzbeks. Evidently reluctant to return to the Safavid court, where Chūha Sulṭān Takkalū was in power, they spent a year moving through Sistan and Baluchistan, using such opportunities for plunder as presented themselves. They then turned to the West and reached Fars. From here, in summer 1531, they finally went to submit to Ṭahmāsp, who, returning from his second campaign to Khurasan, had come south to Isfahan. Evidently it was hoped to deal with the problem of the refugees from Herat. At the summer camp of Kandamān Sām Mīrzā was received by his brother, and separated from his *lala*. Ḥusain Khān, with his Shāmlū attacked Chūha Sulṭān, who was killed in a fight in the King's presence in which arrows narrowly missed the Shah. It was not long before the other tribes joined in to overthrow the dominant Takkalū. Ḥusain Khān and ʻAbdallāh Khān Ustājlū became joint chief amirs.

On the Shah's next campaign to the East, in 1533-4, Sām Mīrzā was again appointed Governor of Herat, with another Shāmlū *lala*, Aghzivār Sulṭān. (They replaced Bahrām Mīrzā and Ghāzī Khān Takkalū.) Ṭahmāsp had received news of the Ottoman invasion and, when doubts were expressed about the loyalty of those to be left at Herat he stated that if they were disloyal it would be better not to have them with him at such a time anyway. When news reached Herat that Ḥusain Khān Shāmlū had been executed by Ṭahmāsp a rebellion was begun. Much remains uncertain about the episode. News of it was given to the Ottoman Sultan Sulaimān by the Takkalū traitors Ulāma, and then Ghāzī Khān, who was apparently in communication with Sām Mīrzā. Sulaimān himself proclaimed in his own camp that Sām was his son, and that he had 'given' him the lands of Iran beyond the Qizil Uzun river. How far Sām Mīrzā, then about eighteen, was a willing participant or a puppet in the hands of the Shāmlū of his nominal following is not known, but, if there was a real plot involving the Ottomans or Qizilbāsh renegades in the West, it is certain no useful degree of co-ordination was ever achieved. Early in 1535 the rebels moved from Herat. The initial intention may have been to proceed westward and threaten Ṭahmāsp, but in the event, moving in the opposite direction, they undertook a siege of the Mughal fortress of Qandahar. After eight months they were defeated by the Mughal Prince Kāmrān in a pitched battle. Aghzīvār Sulṭān was taken prisoner, and put to death. Sām retreated northwest to Ṭabas in Khurasan and, executing a number of his followers, offered his submission to his brother.

The Shah despatched a letter to Ṭabas, giving assurances on oath. The Prince was collected by, among others, Shāh qulī Khalīfa and brought to court. He was taken to the harem and 'treated with favour' but ordered to follow the court attended by a guard of thirty *qūrchīs* drawn from all the Qizilbāsh clans (in order to minimize any chance of plotting). His food and clothing were to be supplied from the Royal Household. It was this ignominious situation that Membré saw him in. The songs proclaiming that Sām was to be put on Sulaimān's throne in Constantinople must have seemed, in fact have been, distinctly ironic, responding as they did to Sulaimān's announcements that Sām was to be made Shah of Persia.

After twelve years Sām Mīrzā submitted that he could no longer bear the hardships of constant travel and asked to be assigned a place to settle. Ṭahmāsp appointed him custodian of the shrine of the ancestors of the Safavid family at Ardabil and governor of the province. He was still closely controlled. He remained in this post until 1561, when he asked to be allowed to retire to

Mashhad. At first the request was accepted, but Ṭahmāsp changed his mind and Sām was sent to the state prison of Qahqaha. There he met his death, together with two of his own sons and two sons of Alqās Mīrzā, in December-January 1567-1568. The *Khulāṣat al-Tavārīkh* gives a detailed account of how Ṭahmāsp arranged to have the Princes put to death, and publicly stated that they had been killed in an earthquake.

Like his brothers Ṭahmāsp and Bahrām, Sām was a man of education and taste. In his youth at Herat he was exposed to the afterglow from the cultured court of the Timurid ruler Sulṭān Ḥusain Bāiqarā. His own court at Ardabil was a centre for the learned, particularly poets. It was there that he completed his biographical dictionary of poets, the *Tuḥfa-yi Sāmī*.

Shāh 'Alī Sulṭān Chapnī. Membré's host in the Royal Camp. We hear again of Shāh 'Alī Sulṭān Chapnī as governor of Van and castellan of its great fort in 1549, when it was surrendered by him to the Ottoman army.

Shāh Ismā'īl. Ṭahmāsp's father, the founder of the Safavid state and its first ruler, 1501-1524.

Shāh qulī Khalīfa. Membré's host at Tabriz, Shāh qulī Khalīfa was of the Qāvurghalū clan of the Dhu 'l-qadar. The tribe had come to Iran from Turkey, from the region of the little Dhu 'l-Qadar kingdom situated around Albistān and Mar'ash. He is first mentioned in 1530, as one of the leaders of the tribe. Three years later he held one of the high positions around the King's person, that of Īshīk-āqāsī-bāshī (see Glossary, *īshīk āqāsī*). At that time he was promoted to be Keeper of the Seal(s) when the former Muhrdār was killed in a fall playing polo in the square in Tabriz on Friday - an accident reportedly brought about by the curses of the theologian Shaikh 'Alī Karakī. He retained this important post until his death. At some time he was also made Governor of Qum, a particularly honourable appointment, owing to the city's possession of the tomb of the Eighth Imam's sister Fāṭima. He appears over a long period in the chronicles on court occasions, participating in campaigns, in command of expeditions, and entrusted with affairs of some delicacy. For instance, when the Shah's favourite sister made a pilgrimage to Mashhad he was in charge of the escort. After Ṭahmāsp removed his capital to Qazvin, Shāh qulī Khalīfa's house was next to the King's palace. He fell ill while leading a campaign against the Turcoman of the Astarabad region and died in July 1558.

The title *khalīfa* (see Glossary) shows that Shāh qulī held formal rank in the Safavid Sufi hierarchy, but it is Membré's account that clearly reveals his role as intermediary with Qizilbāsh enthusiasts from inside Turkey and elsewhere who wished to show their respect to the Shah as a holy and messianic figure, and to acquire relics hallowed by contact with his person. Though the title was apparently not in use at the time it is evident that Shāh qulī was carrying out the duties of the official later known as the Khalīfat al-khulafā, the *khalīfa* of the *khalīfas*. The Khalīfat al-khulafā was second-in-command to the Shah for the affairs of the Sufi order, and in particular was responsible for relations with the Qizilbāsh outside Iran, mainly in Turkey, where their descendants still survive. It was probably his familiarity with the diplomatic issues involved with such contacts that made him seem suitable to look after Membré.

Shāhvirdī Beg, Kachal(?). (Text: Chechie chiavordi, Chechiachaverdi pech) The editors propose *shaikh* or *ḥājjī* for the first element of the name. *Khwāja* might also be considered, but none of these seems really appropriate for a Qizilbāsh officer of the period. A Kachal Shāhvirdī Beg Ustājlū makes his appearance in the chronicles not long after Membré's visit and it is quite likely that he is the person intended. *Kachal* in Persian and Turkish means 'scald-headed', that is having the scalp affected with the unsightly marks of skin disease, typically ring-worm. Such disparaging nicknames were not unknown (cf. Kūpik qirān above).

Kachal Shāhvirdī Beg makes his first appearance in the chronicles in 1544-1545, when he commanded a detachment of *qūrchīs* sent with Humāyūn (q.v.) against Qandahar. In 1550 he became Governor of Astarabad but his amorous attentions to the young chief of the local Turcomans led to a revolt in which he was killed.

Shakkī, Beg of. (Text: Chiachi bech) As noted and further discussed in the entry on the sisters of Ṭahmāsp, a Persian chronicle states that the Lord of Shakkī was married to one of Ṭahmāsp's daughters during the year Membré arrived in Persia. His actual name was Darvīsh Muḥammad, but presumably Membré heard him referred to, in Turkish, as Shakkī Beg[i], the Beg or Amir of Shakkī. Shakkī was a small, but semi-independent, district on the north of Shīrvān, and was indeed very close to the Georgian town of Zagem. After his Safavid wife had died, Ṭahmāsp became dissatisfied with Darvīsh Muḥammad Khān and he was killed in the course of a Safavid campaign against his territory in 1551. Shakkī was then fully incorporated into the Safavid state.

Signor, The. See Turk.

Sophy. See Ṭahmāsp and the entry in the Glossary.

Soprassi, King of Lar. Membré's Soprassi may represent the name Sarfarāz, but in fact the ruler of the still semi-independent kingdom of Lar at the time was Anūshīrvān, also known as Shāh-i 'ādil, meaning 'the just Shah'. It is noteworthy that Membré remarks on the justice of his rule. He had become King in 1524 and was assassinated as he left the Friday Mosque in Lar, probably in June 1541, the year after Membré passed through the town. The Lord of Gilan called Soprasi mentioned earlier is not certainly identified.

Sulaimān Chalabī. Presumably the Sulaimān Chalabī (Çelebi) Chapnī who is mentioned as a commander in the campaign against Alqās Mīrzā in Shīrvān in 1546-1547 and as governor of Urūmī in 1548.

Sulṭān Ḥaidar. Grandfather of Shāh Ṭahmāsp and generally credited with the initial invention of the *tāj*, the distinctive red cap of the Qizilbāsh. Ḥaidar's father Junaid was the first of the Safavids to adopt a policy of militance and met his death as a result, probably in 1460. Ḥaidar was a posthumous child; when he grew up he pursued his father's policies and was himself killed in battle with the forces of the Shīrvānshāh in 1488.

Sulṭān Muṣṭafā. As Membré says, Sulṭān Muṣṭafā was the eldest son of the Turkish Sultan Sulaimān the Magnificent. The capable Prince was long expected to succeed his father but as a result of intrigues by the Sultan's favourite wife Roxalana and the latter's son-in-law Rustam Pāshā he was put to death by Sulaimān in 1553.

Tachiatan Masur. Unidentified, nor is the Persian form of the name obvious, though the second word may be Manṣūr; it is once given as Mansur.

Ṭahmāsp. Second Safavid Shah of Persia. Born 26 Dhu 'l-Ḥijja 918/3 March 1513; reigned 1524-1576.

Ṭahmāsp, Sisters of. The sister said to be destined to be the wife of the Mahdī was Sulṭānim, also known as Mihīn Bānū, the youngest of Shāh Ismā'īl's daughters and born of the same mother as Ṭahmāsp. A remarkable obituary notice is given in the *Khulāṣat al-Tawārīkh*. Her death occurred on 19 February 1562, when she was 44 (lunar) years of age. Her piety and purity were such as to enthral Ṭahmāsp, who dedicated her by vow (*nadhr namūd*) to the Mahdī or Twelfth Imām, consulted her on all state affairs and did not act without her approval, making her 'the Queen of the age, the Mistress of the time'. Elsewhere we hear that scandalous gossip about the relationship between brother and sister was current. Her place as the Mahdī's bride-to-be was later taken by one of Ṭahmāsp's daughters.

Four other sisters of Ṭahmāsp are listed as having survived infancy. As for the two mentioned by Membré, the *Takmilat al-Akhbār* records that in summer 1539, probably not long before Membré arrived at court, the Shah's full sister Parī Khān Khānum was given, in marriage, to Darvīsh Muḥammad Khān, the son of Ḥasan Sulṭān of Shakkī. Darvīsh Muḥammad is evidently Membré's 'King who is near Shīrvān to the north' (see above, under Shakkī, Beg of). The same chronicle attributes the behaviour which led to Ṭahmāsp's dissatisfaction with Darvīsh Muḥammad and his subsequent violent end to the absence of the restraining influence of his Safavid wife, who had died.

Persian sources also confirm that one of Ṭahmāsp's sisters was married to 'Abdallāh Khān Ustājlū (q.v.). Where she is named, however, it is as Parī Khān Khānum and, as just mentioned, according to the *Takmilat al-Akhbār*, the daughter of Ismā'īl married to Darvīsh Muḥammad of Shakkī was called Parī Khān Khānum. Only one Parī Khān Khānum is given in the usual list of Shāh Ismā'īl's daughters. Presumably there is some confusion in the sources. (The most conspicuous Parī Khān Khānum, Ṭahmāsp's daughter, needs to be distinguished from any namesakes.) There does not appear to be any confirmation that Shāh qulī Khalīfa (q.v.) was connected to the Royal Family by marriage.

Ṭahmāsp, Sons of. It seems that in fact Ṭahmāsp had three, rather than two, sons living at the time of Membré's visit. The eldest son, Sulṭān Muḥammad Khudābanda, was born in the winter of 1531-1532. He was, as Membré says, in Khurasan at this time, for in 1537, he had become Governor of Herat. It was the custom of the early Safavids to place Princes in such positions at a very early age; the actual administration was carried out by the Prince's *lala* or tutor, normally a Qizilbāsh amir. Sulṭān Muḥammad spent most of the rest of Ṭahmāsp's reign in Herat. An infection that damaged his eyesight led to his exclusion from the succession at the death of his father in favour of his younger brother Ismā'īl. The latter soon died after killing most of the male members of the Royal family, whereupon Sulṭān Muḥammad did become Shah, reigning 1578-1588.

The second son was Ismā'īl Mīrzā, who was born in Qum in May 1537. One source makes him nominal Governor of Astarābād at about the time of Membré's visit to Persia, with Ṣadr al-Dīn Khān Ustājlū as his *lala*. Ismā'īl grew up to be a forceful character and was imprisoned by his father. However, after many years in Qahqaha castle, he emerged as the winner in the struggle for the throne after Ṭahmāsp's death and reigned briefly and bloodily, 1576-1577.

A third son, Sulṭān Murād Mīrzā is said to have been born in winter 1538-1539. The unfortunate child was sent with the Safavid force that assisted the Mughal Humāyūn (q.v.) to take Qandahār. It was intended that he should nominally govern the town for the Shah after its capture but he very soon died (1545). There is no confirmation that either he or Ismā'īl Mīrzā was in Shiraz or Yazd as Membré thought, nor does it appear particularly likely.

Tājlū Begum. Membré: Tachina pegum. Ṭahmāsp's mother. The name means 'Lady of the *Tāj*' and was on occasion used for other women of the Royal Family. Its precise significance is not established but it seems likely that it implies that the woman concerned was entitled to wear the Qizilbāsh *tāj*, essentially an item of male dress.

Ṭahmāsp himself refers to his mother several times simply as Begum. Her actual name was Shāh Begī Begum. She was the daughter of Mihmād Beg Mauṣillū, and the Mauṣillū were a cadet branch of the Royal Family of the Āqquyūnlū, the dynasty overthrown by Shāh Ismā'īl. Many of the Āqquyūnlū were put to death, but Shāhī Begī, as a young girl, was with a group of refugees who fell into Safavid hands some years after the initial massacres. Some time later she was married to Ismā'īl and became the most beloved and influential of his wives. At the battle of Chāldirān in 1514 she fell briefly into Ottoman captivity but she managed to make her escape. Shortly before this she had borne Ismā'īl his first son, the future Shāh Ṭahmāsp. Bahrām Mīrzā was also her son and she had at least two daughters. In the later years of Ismā'īl's reign her political influence was strong.

After the accession of Ṭahmāsp, Tājlū Begum continued to play a significant political and diplomatic role. She had great financial resources and was responsible for a number of charitable and other works of construction. She was the senior lady of the Royal Harem, though by the time that Membré joined the *urdū* the storm was already under way and she had been left in Tabriz. The plot to poison the Shah and replace him with Bahrām Mīrzā is not mentioned elsewhere. Tājlū Begum's actual banishment is, and is described as due to her continuing to behave as in times past. This is probably to be explained as implying both Ṭahmāsp's personal desire to free himself at last from the pressure of a strong personality, and Tājlū Begum's own understandable reluctance to adapt to the the gradual weakening of the early Qizilbāsh ethos. She was expelled from the Harem and banished to Shiraz, as Membré says. The ride in a *kajāva*, a narrow box-like litter, on an inferior camel must have been a great humiliation. She died soon after arriving in Shiraz.

Turk, The. The Ottoman Sulṭān, at this time Sulaimān the Magnificent, r. 1520-1566. Also referred to as the Signor.

'Ubaid Khān Uzbek. 'Ubaid or 'Ubaidallāh Khān was the ruler of Bukhārā for most of the early 16th century until his death on 18 March 1540. He was Great Khān of the Uzbeks of Transoxiana from 1533. Among the rulers of the loose Uzbek confederation of Transoxiana he was the conspicuous supporter of the policy of expansion into Khurasan, which the Safavids also claimed. This conflict, which was exacerbated by religious differences, was one of the major problems facing the Safavid state at the beginning of Ṭahmāsp's reign. Ṭahmāsp undertook five campaigns to distant Khurasan, reaching Tabriz on his return from the last one early in 1538. He was probably beginning to get the upper hand in the struggle, but in any case, with 'Ubaid Khān's death the pressure was relieved. Though Membré does not mention it the news almost certainly reached the Persian court during the last few months of his stay.

'Umar. The second Caliph (634-644); regarded by the Shi'ites as a usurper. See Abū Bakr.

Uskū, Sayyids of. Membré gives a fascinating glimpse of the Sayyids at the height of their influence. He refers to them in a Turkish form, *Uscup seitler*, and rightly states that there were four of them. They were brothers from the village of Uskū, 10 miles south-west of Tabriz. The Sayyids became favourites of Ṭahmāsp's in 1537-1538, and the Persian acounts indicate that they were favourites of the purest type: people whose merits or charms were concealed from everyone except the source of favour. As Membré indicates, they ranked very high at court and we are told elsewhere that the Shah was exceptionally attentive to them and their wishes and that their advice carried weight. However, even with his favourites, Ṭahmāsp showed his characteristic caution: none of the Sayyids seems to have held an office more influential than that of Key-holder of the Royal Library, enjoyed by the third brother Niẓām al-Dīn Aḥmad. Sām Mīrzā is not alone in referring to their boorish simplicity and incapacity for affairs, though others at Ṭahmāsp's court might well have swallowed Membré's equation of St. Mark and 'Alī equally happily. A year or so after Membré's departure, they fell from favour, Niẓām al-Din Aḥmad supposedly leading a plot for the brothers to win the positions of Vakīl, Ṣadr (superintendent of certain religious affairs) and Muhrdār. The incumbent Vakīl, Qāḍī-yi Jahān, who had supported them in their rise, naturally changed his attitude. The brothers' lack of political weight is shown by the fact that they survived their fall, being merely sent back to Uskū and even allowed to retain the tax-grants (*suyūrghāls*) which they had been given in their period of prosperity.

'Uthmān. The third Caliph (644-656); regarded by the Shi'ites as a usurper. See Abū Bakr.

Uzbek, King of Khwarazm. Membré appears to have taken Uzbek as a personal name here, but in his time it was used as an ethnic or tribal designation, that of the Turkish people who provided the rulers of Transoxiana and Khwarazm, and who were also known as the Green Heads or Green Hats. The Uzbek state of Khwarazm, like that of Transoxiana, was divided among the members of the ruling house into petty kingdoms which acknowledged the senior ruler as Great Khan.

Membré's Uzbek embassies and the associated events are not mentioned in the Persian sources. The current Great Khan of Khwarazm was called Abū Yūsuf, but it is likely that Membré's King was one of the nominally subordinate rulers, Dīn Muḥammad Khān, who was pursuing a pro-Safavid policy and had become conspicuous by his leading role in ending the occupation of part of Khwarazm by the Transoxianan Uzbeks under ʻUbaid Khān (q.v.). This was in 1538 or possibly 1539. At an earlier stage Qizilbāsh forces had driven him and his brother ʻAlī Sulṭān from their territories of Nisā and Abīvard which, on the southern fringes of the Qara Qum Desert, were, as Membré puts it, 'near Khurasan'. They had made their way to the court of Ṭahmāsp, and been appointed Safavid governors of the same territories. A Safavid embassy, like that described by Membré, is known to have been sent to Dīn Muḥammad in response to his report of the defeat and flight of the Transoxianan Uzbeks. The campaign alluded to by Membré is possibly Dīn Muḥammad's capture of Marv from the subordinates of ʻUbaid Khān, described in the chronological confusion of Abu 'l-Ghāzī's account of Khwarazmian history. Dīn Muḥammad's brother ʻAlī Sulṭān is likely to be the person Membré saw.

GLOSSARY

agosatti. so text, glossed, '*zoè molettieri*'.

Greek *agōgiatēs*: carrier, muleteer. *agōgē*: carriage.

'alam(s). text: *alemi.*

Arabic > Persian (Turkish *'alem*): standard. The description of the Safavid standards is confirmed by representations in miniatures and surviving metal standard-tops, but the openwork inscriptions of the tops seem to have normally been much shorter than the one given (see the next item). Usually they simply read, '*Allāh, Muḥammad, 'Alī.*'

'Alī walī Allāh; lā ilāh illā Allāh; 'Alī walī allāh wa Allāhu akbar.

Text: *Alic vali ulla, la illa illa la, alic velli ulla, vulla acpar.*

Arabic: ''Alī is the friend of God; there is no God but God; 'Alī is the friend of God, and God is most great.' See *'alam.*

Allāh, Allāh. Devletlu khūndkār ömrini ziyāde eylesin.

Text: *alla, alla ttoulati conducar embri ziate ilessin.*

Turkish: 'God, God; may He lengthen the life of the Most Fortunate Sultan.' *Khūndkār* (perhaps from Persian *khudāwandgār*, Lord) was a standard title of the Ottoman Sultans.

altun. text: *altun.*

Turkish (> Persian) *altun*: gold, gold coin, corresponding here to Arabic (> Persian, Turkish) *dīnār*, itself from Latin *denarius.* Initially the Islamic *dīnār* was a gold coin and the word never lost that meaning, but in the accounting system used in Persia the 'book' *dīnār* kept losing value, owing to successive diminutions of the weight standard of the coinage. It is this system of money of account that lies behind the use of *altun* for copper coinage. In the accounting system the *shāhī* was rated at 50 *dīnārs* (in Membré's usage 50 *altun*). *Altun* in this sense of book *dīnār* is attested in the 15th century and still to some extent survives in Azeri Turkish. See *shāhī.*

armozeen(s). text: *ormesini.*

A type of light silk cloth. Another Italian form is *ermisini.* It has been suggested that the name derives from that of Hormuz, which would have been the place of import or transhipment rather than production. Applied by Membré to the silk pennants on the royal standards.

'Āshūrā. text: *achiur*, and, in Greek script: *akiour*.

Arabic > Persian, Turkish: the tenth of the month of Muḥarram and the associated ceremonies, marking, especially for the Shi'ites, the commemoration of the death of the Imām Ḥusain.

asper(s). text: *aspri*.

Greek *aspros*: invisible, later white; *aspros*, *aspron*: a silver coin. Italian *aspro* in the meaning of silver coin is no doubt from the Greek, but is affected by the Latin *asper*, rough, which, applied to coin, has the specialized meaning 'new-minted'. Membré uses it for Imeretian and Persian silver and even Persian copper coins, as well as for the asper par excellence of his time, the silver coin of the Ottoman Empire. This last was itself in Turkish called *aqcha*, from *aq*, meaning white, a calque from the Greek.

aznāvur(s). text: *asnauri*.

Georgian *aznauri*: Georgian of the knightly class.

bagatin.

Or *bagattino*. Billon or copper Venetian coin. 12 were worth a soldo and 240 a lira. Which of the varieties Membré has in mind is uncertain.

bandar.

Persian: port.

bairam. text: *bairan*.

Turkish *bairam*: festival, feast day. Membré presumably heard the word in Turkish; it does not seems to have been employed in Persian. The Persian Easter (*pasca*) to which he applies it is likely to be the Persian New Year Festival, Naurūz, celebrated at the spring equinox.

beg.

Turkish *beg* : chief, amir. Used as a title in Persian.

bocasin(s). text: *boccassini*.

From Turkish *boghası*: cotton cloth, much used for linings.

botanoes. text: *bottane*.

From Arabic *biṭāna*, *buṭāna*: lining; coarse cotton or linen cloth.

brigantine. text: *bregantino*, *bregantin*.

At this period, a small vessel equipped with both sails and oars. Apparently smaller than the otherwise similar foist.

bughrā. text: *bogra*.

Turkish *bughra*: male camel, whence Persian *bughrā-khānī* or *bughrā*: a dish made with strips of flour paste, supposedly named after a central Asian ruler called Bughrā Khān. This meaning is also found in Turkish. Several recipes are given in the two Safavid cookery books published by Īraj Afshār. One of these works is from the reign of Shah Ismā'īl, the second from that of Shah 'Abbās (1588-1629); both are concerned with the luxurious cookery of court circles. They greatly help to explain Membré's remarks on Persian food.

camlet(s). text: *zambelloti*.

Light cloth with a pronounced nap, made from the long wool of sheep or the Angora goat. From Arabic *khimla*: cloth with such a nap. Cf. *khaml*: nap, pile. The etymology from Arabic *jamal*, camel, is now rejected. Angora (modern Ankara) was of course the important centre of production.

canarine silk. text: *seda canarine*.

A few Italian sources of the sixteenth century and earlier mention what, allowing for variant spellings, is evidently the same type of silk, and some state it to be produced in the district of Qarābāgh. The apparent locus classicus is in the account of Safavid Persia in the first decade of the sixteenth century by the Anonymous Venetian Merchant (published by Ramusio and in English translation in the Hakluyt Society volume edited by Stanley and Grey): 'Carabasdac [Qarābāgh] is a plain ... in which there is a fine castle, called Canar, which has many villages dependent on it, and where they make the silks which are called Canare, after that place.' However, the castle of Canar appears to be otherwise completely unkown, and so the origin of canarine can not be regarded as settled. Zagem, which Membré identifies as a source of canarine silk, was not situated in Qarābāgh but in Kakhetian Georgia.

chāy. text: *chiai*.

Turkish *chay*: river, stream.

cuirassine. text: *curazina* (sing.), *curazine* (plural).

A coat armoured with small metal plates. The English form is the translator's, on the model of the French. The editors propose a derivation from Persian *khurāsānī*, meaning 'of the province of Khurasan', because Khurasan was supposedly a centre of metal-working, and take it refer to chainmail. But a European origin for cuirassine can be safely accepted, particularly in the absence of evidence that *khurāsānī* was ever used to mean chainmail in Persian. A French passage from 1552, nothing to do with Persia, refers to arquebusiers '*armez de jacques et manches de mailles ou cuirassines*', remarkably close to Membré's second use of the term '*curazine e zachi de maglia*'. Support for this interpretation is provided by the Anonymous Merchant's account of Safavid arms in the time of Ismā'īl which includes the words '*L' armature loro sono corazze di lame indorate, intagliate di bellissimi lavori, & similmente molti giacchi di maglia.*' 'Their armour is cuirasses, of gilded plates, inlaid with the finest work, and, similarly, many coats of mail.' This also makes it apparent that *curazina*/cuirassine means the same as *corazza*/cuirass, that the Persian (and, presumably, Georgian) cuirassines were of lamellar construction rather than of chainmail, and that the cuirasse or cuirassine was an alternative to the coat of mail. For the later sixteenth century Teodoro Balbi (apud Berchet) states that the Persian cuirasse was similar to the European cuirassine (*nostre corazzine*). The derivation is from Latin *corium*, leather.

dārūgha. text: *taruga*.

Mongolian > Persian, Turkish: governor, prefect, police official etc. In the Safavid period the successive capitals, and other major cities, had a *dārūgha* or prefect, whose duties included in particular the maintenance of law and order. The *dārūgha* of the capital was an important official.

dhikr. text: *sicri*.

Arabic > Persian (Turkish *dhikir*): mentioning, remembrance (of God); Sufi ceremony of ecstatic commemoration of God.

dīvānkhāna. text: *divacana*.

Persian *dīvān-khāna*. Used in the Safavid period for the Royal place of audience.

dolman. text: *toloman*.

From Turkish *dolaman*: a long robe with narrow sleeves, open in the front.

dunbak(s). text: *tambuchi*.

Persian *dunbak*, *tunbak*: single-ended drum.

ducat.

Used by Membré for various gold coins. It principally refers to the famous Venetian gold coin which remained in production from its introduction in AD 1284 until the 19th century. The Venetian ducat weighed 3.559g. and was 997/1000 fine, virtually pure gold.

farrāsh. text: *farash*.

Arabic > Persian (Turkish *farrāsh*): male domestic servant, literally 'carpet-spreader'.

fidalgo.

Portuguese: nobleman, gentleman.

foist. text: *fusta*.

Small single-masted vessel, provided with both sails and oars.

fūṭa. text: *futa*.

Arabic > Persian, Turkish *fūṭa*: napkin, towel, cloth.

ghāzībegī. text: *casipeghi*.

Sixteenth-century Persian sources state that the coin called *ghāzībegī* was named after Ghāzī Beg (also Qāḍī Beg), son of the Shīrvānshāh Farrukhyasār, who was himself ruler of Shīrvān in 1501-1503. As a term for various copper coins it remained in use in Persia until the 19th century and survives today in *ghāz*, (cf. *shandarghāz*) used in certain set phrases to signify worthlessness. Cf. farthing.

Green Hats. text: *berette verde* etc.
Translation of Turkish *yeshil-bash*, 'green-headed', used for the Uzbeks of Central Asia, whose green caps contrasted with the red ones of their Qizilbāsh enemies.

Injīl. text: *ingil.*
Arabic > Persian, Turkish *injīl*: the Gospel, the New Testament. From Greek *euangelion.*

İn, Shāh. text: *in chiach.*
'Dismount, by the Shah.' *İn*, Turkish, imperative of *inmek*: to descend, dismount. In the context this seems more likely than that Membré has misunderstood the standard phrase *in shā'a allāh*, 'if God wills.'

ishiq. text: *icechie.*
Turkish *ıshıq*: light, lamp. The kind of torch described by Membré is normally called *mash'al* in Persian.

īshīk-āqāsī. text: *ichich agassi.*
Turkish *ishik-aqası*: chamberlain, literally 'lord of the threshold.' Used at the Safavid court both for those responsible for guarding the royal Ḥaram as described by Membré, and for certain officials charged with the organization and ordering of the King's audiences etc., together with the *yasāvuls* (qq.v.). In the seventeenth century the chief of the Harem guard was called the *Īshīk-āqāsī-bāshī* of the Harem, and has to be distinguished from his more important colleague, the *Īshīk-āqāsī-bāshī* of the *Dīvān*, who had the duty of organizing the details of the King's public life. The latter makes a conspicuous figure in seventeenth century descriptions of Royal audiences. Though this second office appears to have existed by the end of Ṭahmāsp's reign, the position in the early sixteenth-century seems to have been different. It is possible that at the time of Membré's visit there was a single *Īshīk-āqāsī-bāshī*, the one responsible for the Harem, while the official chiefly responsible for the arrangement of audiences and the like was known as the chief *yasāvul* or *yasāvul-bāshī*. (See Farrukhzād Beg in the Biographical Index.)

ka'ba.
The building in the centre of the holy place at Mecca towards which the Muslim turns in praying. Used metaphorically in the letters of the Persian Court to the Doge.

kabāb-i jūja. text: *capap giachia.*
Arabic > Persian (Turkish *kebāb*): grilled meat; Persian *jūja*: young chicken; Persian *kabāb-i jūja*: roast chicken.

kārkhāna. text: *carcanà*.

Persian *kār-khāna*: workshop. Used in the early Safavid period for the workshops, stores etc. which formed part of the Royal court and a substantial portion of which accompanied the king on his travels and campaigns.

kersey(s). text: *carisee*.

Type of coarse woollen cloth, possibly named after the village of Kersey in Suffolk.

khaṭā'ī. text: *catai*; in Greek script: *katai*.

Arabic/Persian *khaṭā'ī*: Cathayan or sinner. The *takhalluṣ* or nom de plume used in his Turkish poems by Shāh Ismā'īl, and by later imitators of the poems. Used by Membré for the poems themselves.

khalīfa. text: *califfa*.

Arabic > Persian, Turkish: *khalīfa*, deputy; applied in the Muslim world to the Caliph as deputy of God, or of his prophet Muḥammad. Also used for the deputies appointed by a Sufi Shaikh, whence its use among the Qizilbāsh for certain officials of the Safavid Sufi organization, appointed by the Shāh in his role as Sufi Shaikh (or by his deputy for the affairs of the organization). Shāh qulī Khalīfa and others who bore the title were *khalīfas* in this sense. It is interesting that Membré also mentions village *khalīfas*. The reference to the Minister Qāḍī-yi Jahān as Ṭahmāsp's *khalīfa* or Caliph is not normal Safavid usage. The correct term for Qāḍī Jahān as minister was *vakīl*; he is also sometimes referred to as vizier.

khanjar. text: *cangiar*.

Persian: dagger.

Lā ilāh illā allāh.

See *'Alī walī allāh* etc. above

lâla. text: *lalà*, glossed '*zoè governador*.'

Persian *lala* > Turkish *lâla*: tutor. Membré only uses the word to describe the tutor of the Ottoman Prince Sulṭān Muṣṭafā. For the early Safavid position of *lala*, referred to a number of times in the biographical notes, see the entry for Ṭahmāsp's sons.

lārī. text: *lari*.

Persian: pertaining to the city of Lar, in southern Persia; currency in the form of a doubled-over piece of thick silver wire, widely used in the Persian Gulf and Indian Ocean in the sixteenth and seventeenth centuries; so called because reputedly first produced at Lār. The established English form is larin. Membré gives what is probably the earliest clear description of the shape of the larin. Larins were struck by the Kings of Hormuz, and also in many other places in the Persian Gulf, India and

Ceylon. In the sixteenth century the larin is stated to have weighed just over 5g.

maidān. text: *meidan*.

Persian: square, playing- or battle-field.

mīrākhur. text: *Mirocar*.

Arabic *amīr* > Persian *mīr*: commander; Persian *ākhur*: stable; Persian *mīr-ākhur*, stable-master, master of horse. In the later Safavid period we know there were two Mīrākhurs, one 'of the bridle (*jilau*)' in charge of the stables at court and the other, 'of the plain (*ṣaḥrā*)', managing the Royal studs.

Mīrzā.

Persian: abbreviated form of *amīr-zāda*, amir's son, prince. Used after the personal name as a title for Princes, and later, before the name, for an educated person or clerk.

mohair(s). text: *mocajari*.

Fine cloth made of the hair of the Angora goat. From Arabic *mukhayyar*, choice (adj.).

mozanigo.

More normally *mocenigo*. A Venetian coin of the lira denomination, bearing a design introduced under Pietro Mocenigo, Doge 1474-1476. It contained 6.18g. of silver, weighed 6.52g., and continued to be strück until 1575.

muhrdār. text: *mucurdar*.

Persian: seal-keeper.

muṣāḥib. text: *musacab*.

Arabic > Turkish, Persian *muṣāḥib*: companion, associate (of the King). Applied as a formal title to certain favoured courtiers at the Safavid court.

muvālī. text: *muvali*.

Arabic *muwālī* > Persian, Turkish *muvālī*: friend, helper. In Shi'ism the believer is under an obligation to be the friend and defender of ʻAlī and the other Imāms, and to absolve himself from the guilt of association with their enemies, by attacking the latter as far as possible. Cf. *tabarrā'ī*, infra.

nadhr. text: *nadir*.

Arabic > Persian *nadhr* (Turkish *nedhir*): a vow, dedication of something by vow.

naft. text: *nafti*.

Arabic/Persian *nafṭ*, *naft*: mineral oil (from the wells at Baku). Cf. Greek *naphtha*, itself of Oriental origin.

naqqāra. text: *naqara*, *nagiara*.

Arabic > Persian,Turkish *naqqāra*: large kettle-drum(s); ceremonial band of the King or others.

nuzl(s). text: *nizille.*

Arabic > Persian, Turkish *nuzl*, *nuzul*: travelling provisions, lodgings.

paigiami.

The text reads *yaigani*, and *paigami* is the editors' emendation (see Scarcia's introduction, n. 80). Persian *pāy*: foot, leg; *jāma*: clothing; *pāijāma*: loose trousers of light cloth. The origin of modern pyjamas. Though a typically Persian formation the word is at home, and most probably originated, in Indian Persian. Despite the fact that Persian miniatures of the period show male figures wearing pyjama-like trousers, often in rather gaudy taste, under their robes, Membré's phrasing, 'as if they are wearing *paigiami* (*como portano paigiami*)', indicates that he had in mind something the Persians did not in fact wear. Presumably he came across the garments in use among the Portuguese and others in the East Indies. This would not be the only case where his vocabulary is influenced by Indo-Portuguese usage. If the emendation is correct Membré's use of the word, to judge by citations in dictionaries, is the earliest European one by over two hundred and fifty years.

parvānachī. text: *parvanachi.*

Persian *parvāna*: authorization, permission; *-chi*: Turkish suffix of agent; Persian *parvānachī*, Turkish *pervānechi*: an official in attendance on a King or Prince whose duty it was to convey his master's verbal orders to the appropriate quarter and see that they were carried out.

pūl. text: *pul.*

Persian *pūl*: money, copper coin, a particular denomination of copper coin.

qaliya pilāv. text: *gaglia pilaf.*

Arabic *qaliya*: frying, a fried dish; Persian *pilāv* (nowadays normally *pulaw*): fried and garnished rice. Two recipes for *qaliya pilāv* are given in the Persian cookery book of the reign of Shah Ismā'īl.

qaliya-yi tursh. text: *galia, turchisim.*

This seems the likely interpretation. *Tursh* means sour, bitter in Persian. The cookery book of Shah 'Abbās's time contains a section on the various types of *qaliya-i tursh*, which are those flavoured with lemon juice, vinegar and similar substances. However, *turchisim* could itself stand for Persian *turshī*: pickles.

qāvurma. text: *kavurman, kavurma.*

Turkish *qavurma*: the act of frying, fried meat (from *qavurmaq*, to fry, parch) > Persian *qāvurma* (modern pronunciation *qurme*): cooked and preserved meat.

qāvurma pilāv. text: *cavurma pilaf.*

Pilaff made with chopped fried meat. 'If well cooked it will not be bad,' according to the later Safavid cookery book.

qibla.

The direction of the Ka'ba at Mecca, towards which the Muslim turns in prayer. Used metaphorically in the letters from the Persian Court to the Doge.

Qizilbāsh. text: *Chisilpech*.

Turkish *qızılbāsh* > Persian: red-headed. Applied to the followers of the Safavids on account of the red cap, the *tāj* (q.v.), which they wore. Cf. *Green hats*, above, and see also the Introduction, in particular, pp. xiv-xvii.

qūrchī. text: *corchi* etc.

Mongolian > Persian (Turkish *qorchi*): bodyguard, guard, man at arms. Originally 'quiver-man', though *qor,* 'quiver', later came to mean arms or armaments in general. Described by Membré as cavalrymen, the *qūrchīs* at this period were the major corps of the standing army, a force of Royal guards selected from the Qizilbāsh as a whole. In contrast to the ordinary Qizilbāsh they received stipends from the central administration. Persian sources occasionally mention *qūrchīs* in the service of princes, like the brother of Qarā khalīfa who, as Membré tells us, was Bahrām Mīrzā's *qūrchī*.

Qūrchībāshī.

Turkish > Persian: *qūrchī-bāshī*, head *qūrchī*, the commander of the corps of *qūrchīs*. See Biographical Notes.

rabāb. text: *ravavà*.

Arabic > Persian, Turkish: rebeck, a kind of stringed instrument resembling a lute or mandolin. A Persian form *ravāva* is also given in the dictionaries. However, Membré describes them as *tamburrini*, that is, tambourines, in the meaning of small drums. He may be misusing the word *rabāb*, but presumably does in fact mean drums, for it is the drums of the defeated foe, rather than his mandolins, that one expects to feature on an occasion like the one he describes.

Rūmīs.

Inhabitants of Rūm, which originally meant the Later Roman, Byzantine Empire. Later used in Persia, as in the letters sent from Ṭahmāsp's court to Venice, to refer to the Ottoman Empire.

Ṣad hazār laʿnat bar ʿUmar, ʿUthmān, Abū Bakr. text: *set casar nealet per Omar, Ottoman, Ebu Bekr*.

Persian: A hundred thousand curses on ʿUmar, ʿUthmān and Abū Bakr (qq.v.).

Nowadays *na'lat* for *la'nat* is a characteristically Azerbaijani mispronunciation, so *nealet* may be a faithful rendering of what was heard.

sanjaq. text: *sangiach*.

Turkish *sanjaq*: flag, district, district governor (the last more fully Sanjaq Bey).

sārī pilāv. text: *saripilaf*.

Turkish *sarı:* yellow; Persian *pilāv*: fried rice. *Sārī pilāv*: pilaff coloured and flavoured with saffron. A recipe for *sārī pilāw* is given in the cookery book from the time of Shah 'Abbās. In that of Ismā'īl's period a similar dish is called *zard pilāv* (Persian *zard*: yellow). The corresponding modern dish is called *za'farān pulau*: saffron pilaff.

ṣarrāf(s). text: *serafi*.

Arabic > Persian, Turkish *ṣarrāf*: money-changer, shroff.

sāyabān. text: *saivan*.

Persian (> Turkish) *sāya-bān*, *sāyavān*: awning, shade.

sayyid. text: *segit*, *segiti*, *segisi*.

Arabic > Persian (Turkish *seyyid*): originally 'lord', later applied as a title to descendants of the prophet Muḥammad, particularly through his grandson Ḥusain.

sazo.

Venetian form for Italian *saggio*, from Latin *exagium*. Among other things it meant the sixth of an ounce and a standard weight for checking coinage. However, it is not clear which unit of weight is intended. The *shāhī* of the time weighed 4.6g., which would imply a *sazo* of 3.07g.

scarlet. text: *scarlatto*.

The English and Italian words may ultimately derive from Persian *saqlāt*, *saqlātūn*, which refer to some type of rich cloth. In Membré's time the term was used for woollen broadcloth, such as was manufactured in England. Such cloth was not necessarily scarlet in colour.

Shāh bāsh. text: *chiach pach*.

From Membré's translation it is evident that he took *bāsh* to be the Turkish word for head, but without a copular *Shāh bash* can hardly mean 'The King is head.' Presumably he heard the expression *Shābāsh*, Persian in origin and found also in Turkish. This is an benedictory expression of joyous approval, particularly appropriate to weddings, which is where Membré himself noted it. It is usually explained as coming from *shād bāsh*, 'be joyful.'

Shāh bāshı ichin. text: *chiachi pachichi*.

Turkish: by the Shah's head.

Shāh destūri. text: *chiach testuri*.

Turkish: (in) the Shah's fashion. Persian *dastūr* > Turkish *destūr*: manner, fashion.

Shāh murādın versin. text: *chiach morati versi*.

Turkish: May the Shah grant your desire.

shāhī. text: *chiachi*.

Persian *shāhī*: pertaining to the Shah; a denomination of Persian silver coin. The *shāhī* was introduced by Ismā'īl. Subsequently it was often reduced in weight and at the time Membré was in Persia it weighed 4.6g. In money of account the *shāhī* was equivalent to 50 *dīnārs*. See *altun*, above.

shāṭir. text: *chiatir*.

Arabic > Persian (Turkish: *shāṭır*) cunning, courier, running footman.

shūrbā. text: *chiorvan*.

Persian *shūrbā* (> Turkish *çorba*): soup, broth. For recipes see the cookery book of Shāh 'Abbās's reign.

Signory, The.

Strictly speaking the Doge of Venice and his Council of Six, but often used for the Venetian Government.

sipāhī(s). text: *spachì*.

Persian > Turkish: military, soldier. In the Ottoman army the term applied, properly, to the 'feudal' cavalry which was supported by grants of the right to the taxes of districts in which they resided.

Sophian(s). text: *sofiani* etc.

This rare and obsolete word is in the *Oxford English Dictionary* under Sufian as well as Sophian. In the absence of a more attractive alternative, it has been revived here to render Membré's *sofiani*, which is found in other Italian writers of the first half of the sixteenth century. In origin it means, as Membré says, men of the Sophy (q.v., below) but in his usage, and that of others, it is the standard term used for the inhabitants of Persia; the term belongs very much to the period when the dominant force in the state was the Sophy's Qizilbāsh following. The only people Membré calls Persians are the clock-maker and the mountebanks in Tabriz.

Sophy, The. The Shah of Persia.

The *O.E.D.* disagrees, but there can be no doubt that in origin Sophy is directly derived from the originally Arabic word *ṣūfī*. In the contemporary Syrian and Egyptian notices of Ismā'īl's early activities, the still mysterious leader of the Qizilbāsh movement is referred to as Ismā'īl the Ṣūfī or simply as the Ṣūfī (Arabic *al-ṣūfī*). From Turkey too similar usages are recorded. The term was rapidly taken up by Europeans, notably the Venetians. Europe, however, not understanding the implications of the term or the reasons for its initial use, continued to employ it as the distinctive designation of the Safavid Shahs, undeterred by occasional objections from those who had been in Persia and gained the impression that the Shah might not regard it as very complimentary.

Ṣūfī is of course derived from *ṣūf*, wool, and was the name given to Islamic mystics because they wore distinctive woollen cloaks. In mediaeval Islam Sufi mysticism was widespread and the Safavid Shahs themselves, as has been pointed out in the Introduction, were descendants of a line of Sufi leaders. After Ismā'īl's rise to power the organization and ideology of the Safavid state continued to retain many Sufi features, orthodox and unorthodox. Right to the end the Safavid Shahs did claim to be Shaikhs, and Sufis.

Nevertheless, Sufi on its own was never a title of great honour in Persian. The survival of Sophy in Europe was presumably assisted by confusion with Ṣafawī, the family name of the dynasty which derives from the name Ṣafī al-Dīn and has no true etymological connection with *ṣūfī*. The spelling Sophy, standard in English and paralleled in other European languages, was no doubt favoured by the existence of Greek *sophos*, wise, and its derivatives.

sufrachī. text: *sufrachissi*.

Arabic *sufra*: (table-) cloth; Turkish *-chi*:suffix of agent; > Turkish *sofrachı* > Persian *sufrachī*: table-steward.

ṣuḥbat. text: *socpeti, socpetti*.

Arabic > Persian (Turkish *ṣoḥbet*): company, conversation; in sixteenth and seventeenth century Persia also: feast, festivity, party, which is evidently how the term was used to Membré. This meaning appears to have fallen out of use.

Sulṭān.

In early sixteenth-century Persia a title granted by the Shah to Qizilbāsh governors and other grandees. Later tends to lose ground to Khān.

Sulṭān-Ḥaidarī. text: *sultan caidari*.

The early form of the characteristic Qizilbāsh cap or *tāj* as introduced by Ṭahmāsp's grandfather, Sulṭān Ḥaidar. Under Shāh Ismā'īl a much taller version of the *tāj* was introduced, which was the normal type at the time of Membré's visit. We owe our knowledge of the name of the *Sulṭān-Ḥaidarī* and its continued use in informal contexts to Membré. See the sketch on page 26.

sulṭānī text: *Sultani.*

Arabic: pertaining to the Sultan; here, a gold coin, compared by Membré to Persian gold issues. Most probably the Ottoman *fındıqlı*, struck in imitation of the Venetian ducat.

sum.

Load of a pack-animal; unit of weight.

tabarrā'ī. text: *teperrari, teperrai.*

From Arabic *tabarra'a*, to release oneself, absolve oneself from guilt. In Shi'ism *tabarru'*, clearance from guilt, means in particular to dissociate oneself from the enemies of the Twelve Imāms, that is in particular the Sunnis, and is a religious duty. The Persian form for the agent, *tabarrā'ī*, derives from the non-classical form of the verbal noun current in Persian, *tabarrā* rather than *tabarru'*. In the sixteenth century professional *tabarrā'īs* were employed whose principal task was to publicly curse the supposed enemies of the Imāms, in particular the first three Caliphs, Abū Bakr, 'Umar and 'Uthmān. Membré's is the fullest description of the institution.

tabarruk. text: *teperiach.*

Arabic > Persian (Turkish *teberrük*): blessing, blessedness, blessed object, especially one that comes from a holy man.

takya-namad. text: *teche nemo.*

Arabic *takya*: reclining; Persian *namad*: felt; *takya-namad*: felt bolster to lean against. The Persian chronicles favour the alternative: *namad-takya*.

tāj. text: *tachi* etc.

Persian *tāj*: crown; in particular the red cap which gave the followers of the Safavids the name Qizilbāsh, 'Red-heads'. Some of Membré's forms of the word are not quite what would be expected and for that reason the Italian editors prefer to take the word as *ṭāqiya*, which also means cap, but is sometimes contrasted with *tāj*. Possibly Membré confused the two words, but it is unlikely that he totally overlooked the distinctive term for a very visible and significant item of Safavid culture, which he describes in detail.

tanka. text: *tangua, tanqua.*

Persian and Turkish: probably derived ultimately from Sanskrit *ṭañka*, meaning a particular weight and thence a coin of that weight. From the fourteenth century applied in Central Asia, Persia, Turkey, India etc. to various silver, and also later copper, coins, including the *lārī* (q.v.).

tannūr. text: *tentur.*

Arabic > Persian: *tannūr* (Turkish *tennur*): normally, oven. Applied by Membré to the underground braziers used in winter at Tabriz. The forms *tantūr*, *tandūr* are also found in Persian and Turkish sources, and Membré evidently heard some such variant.

techerech (?)

A large, strong kind of camel. The editors suggest that Membré's word may represent Persian *bīsurāk*, which means a young cross-bred camel.

tūmān(s). text: *tumani*.

Turkish *tümen* > Persian *tūmān*, *tuman*: ten thousand, ten thousand *dīnārs* (money of account). See *altun*. An ultimate origin from Tocharian has been suggested.

ūkyāy qūrchīsī. text: *ochiagi corsichin*.

Turkish *ok-yay qorchisi*: *qūrchī* of the bow and arrow. See *qūrchī*. In Persian sources the equivalent *qūrchī-yi tir u kamān* occurs, as the senior of a group of *qūrchīs* entrusted with the care of items of the Shāh's arms, clothing etc. Occasional references in chronicles support Membré's statement that each Lord had his own *ūkyāy qūrchīsī*. They can be seen in contemporary miniatures.

urdū. text: *(h)ordu*.

Turkish *ordu* > Persian *urdū*: (royal) encampment. Cf. English *horde*.

utāq. text: *ottach*.

Eastern Turkish > Persian: *utāq*, *uṭāq*: tent, Prince's tent (in modern Persian: room). Applied to tents of the trellis-framed, felt-covered type with dome-shaped roof which was used principally by nomads of Turkish and Mongolian origin.

Vedor de fazenda. text: *viador della facenda*, glossing '*il vice-governador*'.

Portuguese: Title of the Superintendent of Revenue in Portuguese India, who ranked second to the Governor.

yasāvul(s). text: *diassagoli* etc.

Turkish *yasā* + Mongolian suffix of agent > Persian, Turkish: *yasāvul*: bodyguard, chamberlain, marshall, usher. From Turkish *yāsā/yāsāq*, law, command. The *yasāvuls* described by Membré were among the court officials who ensured the good order and smooth running of affairs in the King's presence, particularly in public audiences. As Membré notes, they carried a stick as their badge of office. As he also notes, there was a small group of higher-ranking *yasāvuls*. These were known as *yasāvulān-i ṣuḥbat*, *yasāvuls* of the (Royal) company, i.e. of the Presence, or 'of Honour'. They were stationed close to the king, would summon people to his presence, see that what he wanted was fetched and so on. Membré made a number of particular friends among this group.

yasāqī. text: *diasachi*.

Turkish > Persian *yasāqī* (or perhaps *yasāqchī*): guard. From Turkish *yāsā/yāsāq*, law, command, like *yasāvul*. From Pietro Della Valle we learn that in the time of Shah 'Abbās the term was applied to the soldiers who guarded the rear of the Royal Harem while it was on the move. These men wore as the sign of their office an arrow stuck upright, feathers upward, in the front of their turbans. The arrow of their commander, the Yasāqī-bāshī, was of gold. Qarā Khalīfa's brother, who is described by Membré as Bahram Mīrzā's *yasāqī,* wore the same insignia and was probably therefore in charge of guarding the Prince's womenfolk on journeys and in camp, and perhaps at other times as well.

Yazīd. text: *giesiet.*

Yazīd was the name of the second Umayyad Caliph (r. AD 680-683), who was responsible for the persecution of the Imām Ḥusain and his family, and who is therefore particularly detested by the Shi'ites. Membré speaks of Yazīd as a certain race (*certa generazion*) and was evidently not fully aware of the details of the story of the death of Ḥusain. The Safavid custom of referring to enemies by the Turkish plural *Yezidler,* as Shāh Ismā'īl does in his poetry, is the likely source of his interpretation.

zabīb. text: *zibibo.*

Arabic > Persian (Turkish *zebīb*): currant.

BIBLIOGRAPHY

Membré, Michele, *Relazione di Persia (1542)*, Istituto Universitario Orientale, Napoli 1969.

Ms. inedito dell' Archivio di Stato di Venezia pubblicato da Giorgio R. CARDONA. Con una appendice di documenti coevi, concernenti il primo quindicennio di regno dello Scià Ṭahmāsp (1525-40), a cura di Francesco CASTRO. Indici di Angelo M. PIEMONTESE. Presentazione di Gianroberto SCARCIA.

* * *

'Abdī Beg Shīrāzī, *Takmilat al-Akhbār*, ed. 'Abd al-Ḥusain Navā'ī, Tehran 1369.

Abu 'l-Ghāzī, *Histoire des Mogols et des Tatares*, ed. and trans. le baron Desmaisons, St. Petersburg 1871-4.

Afshār, Īraj (ed.), *Āshpazī-yi Daura-yi Ṣafaviyya*, Tehran 1360.

Allen, W.E.D., *A History of the Georgian People*, London 1932.

Allen, W.E.D., *Russian Embassies to the Georgian Kings (1589-1605)*, Cambridge 1970.

Almagià, R., 'A proposito del mappamondo in lingua turca della biblioteca Marciana', *Atti dell' Istituto Veneto di Scienze, Lettere ed Arti*, vol. cxviii, 1959-60, Classe di science morali e lettere, pp. 53-9.

Amīr Maḥmūd b. Khwāndamīr, *Tārīkh-i Shāh Ismā'īl va Shāh Ṭahmāsp*, British Library MS Or. 2,939.

Amīr Maḥmūd b. Khwāndamīr, *Īrān dar Rūzgār-i Shāh Ismā'īl va Shāh Ṭahmāsb-i Ṣafavī*, ed. Ghulām-Riḍā Ṭabāṭabā'ī, Tehran 1370.

Andrews, Peter Alford, *The Felt Tent in Middle Asia. The Nomadic Tradition and its Interaction with Princely Tentage*, Ph. D. Thesis, School of Oriental and African Studies, University of London, 1980.

Anon., *A Chronicle of the Carmelites in Persia*, London 1939.

Arjomand, Said Amir, *The Shadow of God and the Hidden Imam*, Chicago 1984.

Aubin, Jean, 'La politique religieuse des Safavides', *Le Shî'isme imâmite. Colloque de Strasbourg*, Paris 1970, pp. 235-44.

Aubin, Jean, 'L' avènement des Safavides reconsidéré', *Moyen Orient & Océan Indien*, v (1988), pp. 1-130.

Baiao, António (ed.), *Itinerários da Índia a Portugal por terra*, Coimbra 1925.

Berchet, Guglielmo, *La Repubblica di Venezia e la Persia*, Turin 1865.

Boerio, G., *Dizionario del dialetto veneziano*, Venice 1865.

Bombaci, A., 'Ancora sul trattato turco-veneto del 2 ottobre 1540', *Rivista degli Studi Orientali*, xx (1943), pp. 373-81.

Bombaci, A., 'Una lettera turca in caratteri latini del dragomanno ottomano Ibrāhīm al veneziano Michele Membré (1567)', *Rocznik Orientalistyczny*, xv (1949), pp. 129-44.

Bonelli, L., 'Il trattato turco-veneto del 1540', *Centenario della nascita di Michele Amari*, Palermo 1910, ii, pp. 332-63.

The Cambridge History of Iran, vi, ed. P. Jackson and L. Lockhart, Cambridge 1986.

Castanheda, Fernão Lopes de, *Historia do descobrimento e conquista de India pelos Portugueses*, Coimbra 1924-1938.

M.A. Cook (ed.), *A History of the Ottoman Empire to 1730*, Cambridge 1976.

Correa, Gaspar, *Lendas da India*, Lisbon 1858-64.

Couto, Diogo do, *Décadas de Ásia ...*, Lisbon 1736.

Couto, Diogo do, *Década Quinta da "Ásia"*, ed. Marcus de Jong, Coimbra 1936.

Dalgado, A.S., *Glossario Luso-Asiático*, Coimbra 1919-21.

Dānishpazhūh, Muḥammad Taqī, '*Dastūr al-Mulūk-i Mīrzā Rafī'ā va Tadhkirat al-Mulūk-i Mīrzā Samī'ā* ', *Majallah-i Dānishkadah-i Adabiyyāt wa 'Ulūm-i Insānī-yi Dānishgāh-i Tihrān*, xv (1347), pp. 475-504, xvi (1348), pp. 62-93, 298-322, 416-440, 540-563.

Della Valle, Pietro, *I Viaggi. Lettere dalla Persia*, i, ed. F. Gaeta and L. Lockhart, Rome 1972.

Dickson, Martin B., *Sháh Ṭahmásb and the Úzbeks*, Ph. D. Dissertation, Princeton 1958.

Dickson, Martin B., and Stuart C. Welch, *The Houghton Shahnameh*, Cambridge Mass. and London 1981.

Doerfer, Gerhard, *Türkische und Mongolische Elemente in Neupersischen*, Wiesbaden 1963-75.

Faḍlī Iṣfahānī, *Afḍal al-Tavārīkh*, ii, British Library MS Or. 4,678.

Farīdūn b. Aḥmad, *Munsha'āt al-Salāṭīn*, Istanbul 1274-5.

Fehmi, Edhem and Ivan Stchoukine, *Les Manuscrits Orientaux Illustrés de la Bibliothèque de l'Université de Stamboul*, Paris 1933.

Fekete, L., *Einführung in die Persische Paläographie*, ed. G. Hazai, Budapest 1977.

Ghaffārī Qazvīnī, Qāḍī Aḥmad, *Tārīkh-i Jahānārā*, Kitāb-furūshī-yi Ḥāfiẓ, 2nd ed. [Tehran, n.d.].

Hakluyt, Richard, *The Principall Navigations Voiages and Discoveries of the English Nation*, reprint, Cambridge 1965.

Hammer, Joseph von, *Geschichte des Osmanischen Reiches*, Pest 1827-35.

Haneda, Masashi, *Le Châh et les Qizilbâš. Le système militaire safavide*, Berlin 1987.

Iskandar Munshī, *Tārīkh-i 'Ālamārā-yi 'Abbāsī*, ed. Īraj Afshār, Tehran 1334-5.

Jauhar Āftābachī, *Tadhkirat al-Vāqi'āt*, British Library MS Add. 16,711; trans. Major Charles Stewart, London 1832.

Javād-Mashkūr, Muḥammad, *Tārīkh-i Tabrīz tā Pāyān-i Qarn-i nuhum-i Hijrī*, [Tehran] 1352.

Jazarī, Ibn al-Razzāz al-, *The Book of Knowledge of Ingenious Mechanical Devices*, trans. Donald R. Hill, Dordrecht and Boston 1974.

Junābadī, Mīrzā Beg b. Ḥasan Ḥasanī, *Rauḍat al-Ṣafaviyya*, British Library MS Or. 3,388.

Khwāndamīr, *Ḥabīb al-Siyar*, Bombay 1857.

Khwurshāh b. Qubād al-Ḥusainī, *Tārīkh-i Īlchī-yi Niẓāmshāh*, British Library MS. Or. 153.

Lockhart, L., R. Morozzo della Rocca, M.F. Tiepolo (edd.), *I Viaggi in Persia degli Ambasciatori Veneti Barbaro e Contarini*, Rome 1973.

Mas Latrie, M.L. de, *Histoire de l'Ile de Chypre sous le règne des Princes de la maison de Lusignan*, Paris 1852-61.

Ménage, V.L., '"The Map of Hajji Ahmed" and its makers', *Bulletin of the School of Oriental and African Studies*, xxi (1958), pp. 291-314.

Mestre Affonso, *Ytinerario*. See Baiao.

Minorsky, V. (ed.), *Tadhkirat al-Mulūk*, London 1943.

Morgan, E. Delmar and C.H. Coote, *Early Voyages and Travels to Russia and Persia by Anthony Jenkinson and other Englishmen, ...*, London 1886.

Morton, A.H., 'The Ardabīl Shrine in the reign of Shāh Ṭahmāsp I', *Iran*, xii (1974), pp. 31-64; xiii (1975), pp. 39-58.

Morton, A.H., 'The *chūb-i ṭarīq* and Qizilbāsh ritual in Safavid Persia', in *Études Safavides*, ed. Jean Calmard (Paris and Tehran 1993), pp. 225-45.

Mudarrisī Ṭabāṭabā'ī, H., *Turbat-i Pākān*, Qum, Anno Shahinshahi [25]35.

Navā'ī, 'Abd al-Ḥusain, *Shāh Ṭahmāsb-i Ṣafavī, Majmū'a-yi Asnād va Mukātibāt-i Tārīkhī...*, [Tehran] 1351.

Papadopoli (Aldobrandini), Nicolò, *Le Monete di Venezia*, Venice 1893-1919.

Palombini, Barbara von, *Bündniswerben Abendländischer Mächte um Persien 1453-1600*, Wiesbaden 1968.

Qummī, Qāḍī Aḥmad Ḥusainī, *Khulāṣat al-Tavārīkh*, ed. Iḥsān Ishrāqī, Tehran 1980-84.

Qummī, Qāḍī Aḥmad Ḥusainī, *Gulistān-i Hunar*, ed. Aḥmad Suhailī Khwānsārī, [Tehran] 1359; trans., V. Minorsky, *Calligraphers and Painters*, Washington 1959.

Ramusio, G-B., *Le Navigationi et Viaggi*, ii, Venice 1559.

Riazul Islam, *Indo-Persian Relations: a Study of the Political and Diplomatic Relations between the Mughal Empire and Iran*, Tehran 1970.

Riazul Islam, *A Calendar of Documents on Indo-Persian Relations, (1500-1750)*, Karachi 1979-82.

Robinson, B.W. (ed.), *Islamic Art in the Keir Collection*, London 1988.

Röhrborn, K-M, *Provinzen und Zentralgewalt Persiens im 16. und 17. Jahrhundert*, Berlin 1966.

Rūmlū, Ḥasan, *Aḥsan al-Tavārīkh*, [Vol. xii], ed. and trans. C.N. Seddon, Baroda 1931-4.

Rūmlū, Ḥasan, *Aḥsan al-Tavārīkh*, [Vol. xii], ed. 'Abd al-Ḥusain Navā'ī, Intishārāt-i Bābak [Tehran] 1357.

Sām Mīrzā, *Tuḥfah-yi Sāmī*, ed. Rukn al-Dīn Humāyūn-farrukh, Elmi Press [Tehran, n.d.].

Sarwar, Ghulām, *History of Shāh Ismā'īl Ṣafawī*, Aligarh 1939.

Savory, Roger M., 'The principal offices of the Ṣafawid state during the reign of Ṭahmāsp I (930-84/1524-76)', *Bulletin of the School of Oriental and African Studies*, xxiv (1961), pp. 65-85.

Savory, Roger M., 'The Office of *Khalīfat al-Khulafā* under the Ṣafawids', *Journal of the American Oriental Society*, lxxxv (1965), pp. 497-502.

Scarcia, G., 'Un documento persiano del 946/1539 nell' Archivio di Stato di Venezia', *Annali. Istituto Orientale di Napoli*, New Series xviii (1968), pp. 338-42.

Shāh Ṭahmāsp, *Tadhkira-yi Shāh Ṭahmāsp*, ed. D.C. Phillott, Calcutta 1912; ed. 'Abd al-Shukūr, Berlin 1342.

Sharaf Khān Bidlīsī, *Sharaf-nāma*, ed. V. Véliaminof-Zernof, St. Petersburg 1860-2.

Sharaf Khān Bidlīsī, *Sharaf-nāma*, ed. M. 'Abbāsī, [Tehran 1343].

Sharaf Khān Bidlīsī, *Sharaf-nāma*, French translation, *Chèrèf-nâma ou fastes de la nation kurde*, François Bernard Charmoy, St. Petersburg, 1868-75.

Spagni, E., 'Una sultana veneziana', *Nuovo Archivio Veneto*, xix (1900), pp. 244-348.

Stanley of Alderley, Lord and Charles Grey, *Travels to Tana and Persia by Josafa Barbaro and Ambrogio Contarini* and *A Narrative of Italian Travels in Persia in the Fifteenth and Sixteenth Centuries*, London 1873.

Sümer, Faruk, *Safevî Devletenin Kuruluşu ve Gelimişinde Anadolu Türklerinin Rolü*, Ankara 1976.

Tenreiro, António, *Itinerario*. See Baiao.

Tournefort, Joseph P. de, *Voyage d'un botaniste*, ed. Stéphane Yerasimov, Paris 1982.

Whiteway, R.S., *The Rise of the Portuguese Power in India*, Westminster 1899.

Wilber, Donald N., *The Architecture of Islamic Iran. The Ilkhānid Period*, Princeton 1965.

Yule, Henry and A.C. Burnell, *Hobson-Jobson*, ed. William Crooke, London 1903.

INDEX